Portrait of the ALASKA RAILROAD

Text by Kaylene Johnson ★ Photography by Roy Corral

ALASKA NORTHWEST BOOKS®

ANCHORAGE ★ PORTLAND

To my parents, Joe and Gisela Cartmill, who,
from the beginning, set me on the right track.
                              — K. J.

Text © 2003 by Kaylene Johnson
Photographs © 2003 by Roy Corral, unless otherwise credited

Library of Congress Cataloging-in-Publication Data

Johnson, Kaylene, 1961–
    Portrait of the Alaska railroad / text by Kaylene Johnson; photography by Roy Corral.
        p. cm.
    Includes bibliographical references and index.
    ISBN 0-88240-552-7
    1. Alaska Railroad. 2. Alaska—Description and travel.
I. Title.
    TF 25.A4 J64 2003
    385'.09798—dc21   2002026285

PHOTOGRAPHS: Cover: The distinctive blue-and-gold colors of the engines and cabooses instill pride in the hearts of Alaskans; Title page: Touring along Turnagain Arm; Contents page: The single-line route crosses multiple rivers, such as the Nenana in the Interior; Page 4: The Anchorage rail yard; Page 96: End of the Alaska Railroad main line.

OTHER PHOTO CREDITS: Page 10 photos © Kaylene Johnson; Page 26 photo courtesy Alaska State Library, Alaska Purchase Centennial Commission, PCA 20-180; Page 28 photo courtesy Anchorage Museum of History and Art, Alaska Railroad Collection, BL79-2-7635; Page 31 photo courtesy Anchorage Museum of History and Art, ARR Collection, B83-146-13; Pages 32–33 photo courtesy Anchorage Museum of History and Art, ARR Collection 96-15-1; Page 37 photo courtesy Anchorage Museum of History and Art, ARR Collection B70-62-7; Page 56 photo courtesy Anchorage Museum of History and Art, ARR Collection, BL 79-2-4744; Page 57 photo courtesy Anchorage Museum of History and Art, ARR Collection, BL 79-2808; Page 78 photo © Alaska Nellie Historical Society, used with permission.

Alaska Northwest Books®
An imprint of Graphic Arts Center Publishing Company
P.O. Box 10306, Portland, Oregon 97296-0306
503/226-2402 ★ www.gacpc.com

President: Charles M. Hopkins
Associate Publisher: Douglas A. Pfeiffer
Editorial Staff: Timothy W. Frew, Tricia Brown,
   Jean Andrews, Kathy Howard, Jean Bond-Slaughter
Production Staff: Richard L. Owsiany, Joanna Goebel
Editor: Linda Gunnarson
Designer: Amanda Brannon
Cartographer: Gray Mouse Graphics

Printed in Hong Kong

Contents

Workhorses of the Northernmost Line

- The oldest piece of Alaska Railroad rolling stock is a flatcar built in 1915. It is currently used as a boom tender for a locomotive crane.
- Old Number 1, the antique locomotive installed near the entrance to the Anchorage Depot, helped to build the Panama Canal before it was shipped to Alaska.
- The most modern locomotive on the road is the SD70MAC. These 4000 series locomotives have the latest 16-710 turbocharged engines.
- It takes a three-unit "consist" (a term railroaders use for several connected locomotives working together) of the most powerful locomotives to pull an eight-thousand-ton coal train from Healy to Seward.
- On the steepest ruling grade (3 percent) between Spencer and Grandview, the consist takes thirty-two cars up and over the hill to the Hunter station, and

then returns for the remaining thirty-three cars. The sixty-five-car train is then reassembled at Hunter for the rest of the trip to Seward. Depending on conditions, the same "doubling the hill" procedure is sometimes used from Snow River to Divide. Both areas are south of Anchorage in the Kenai Mountains.

- The Museum of Alaska Transportation and Industry features a railroad exhibit with a collection of old Alaska Railroad locomotives and rolling stock. Steam locomotive cranes, a Jordan Spreader, Pullman cars, and other equipment are on display at the twenty-acre site north of Wasilla. The museum also has a section house, a wooden caboose, and railroad equipment used by the military. For more information about the museum and details about specific railroad artifacts, visit their Web site at www.alaska.net/~rmorris/mati1.htm or call (907) 376-3082.

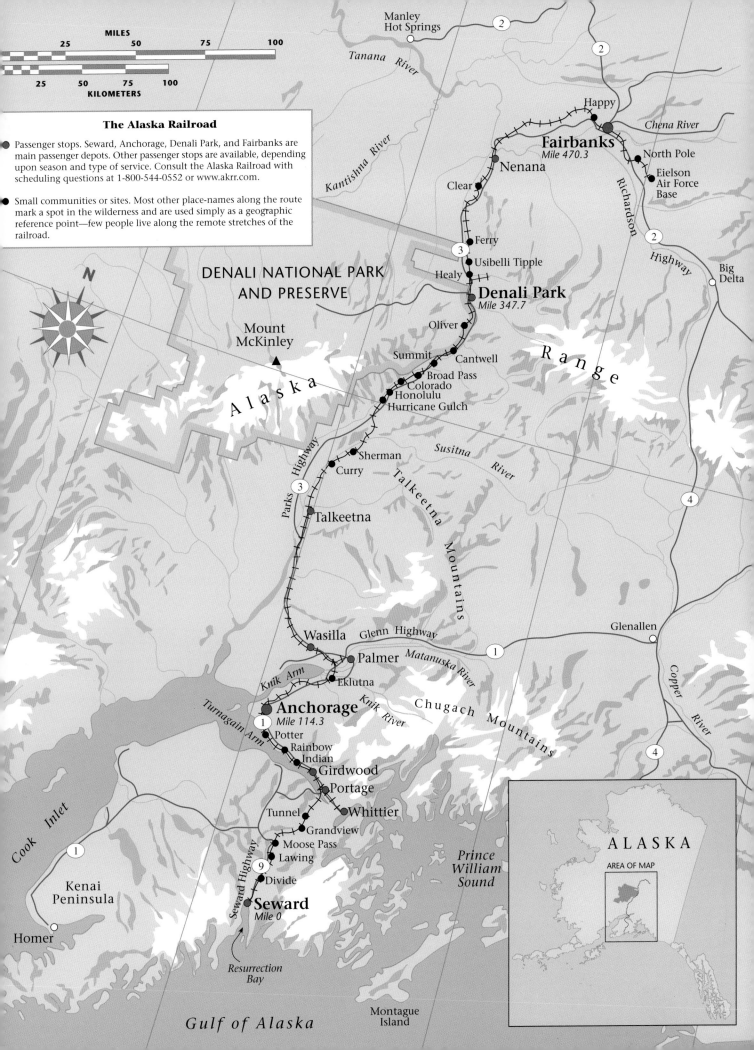

MILES
25 50 75 100

25 50 75 100
KILOMETERS

The Alaska Railroad

● Passenger stops. Seward, Anchorage, Denali Park, and Fairbanks are main passenger depots. Other passenger stops are available, depending upon season and type of service. Consult the Alaska Railroad with scheduling questions at 1-800-544-0552 or www.akrr.com.

● Small communities or sites. Most other place-names along the route mark a spot in the wilderness and are used simply as a geographic reference point—few people live along the remote stretches of the railroad.

Manley Hot Springs

Tanana River

Kantishna River

Clear

Nenana

Happy

Fairbanks
Mile 470.3

Chena River

North Pole

Eielson Air Force Base

Richardson Highway

Big Delta

DENALI NATIONAL PARK AND PRESERVE

Ferry

Usibelli Tipple

Healy

Denali Park
Mile 347.7

Oliver

Mount McKinley

Summit

Cantwell

Broad Pass

Colorado

Honolulu

Hurricane Gulch

R a n g e

A l a s k a

Sherman

Curry

Susitna River

Talkeetna

Talkeetna Mountains

Parks Highway

Wasilla

Glenn Highway

Palmer

Matanuska River

Glenallen

Eklutna

Knik Arm

Knik River

Anchorage
Mile 114.3

Chugach Mountains

Copper River

Potter

Turnagain Arm

Rainbow

Indian

Girdwood

Portage

Whittier

Tunnel

Grandview

Prince William Sound

Moose Pass

Lawing

Seward Highway

Divide

Cook Inlet

Kenai Peninsula

Seward
Mile 0

Homer

Resurrection Bay

Gulf of Alaska

Montague Island

A L A S K A

AREA OF MAP

Chapter One

"The Ties That Bind Alaska"

ALASKA'S TRAINS CAPTURE ALL THE ROMANCE OF MY CHILDHOOD MEMORIES—
and more. Where I grew up in North Dakota, a lonely train whistle announced the end of
each day. Sounding shortly after dark, the whistle seemed a lonesome call from a distant place.
At once it was the sound of the past and the future, of places too far away to imagine.

Living in Alaska, I discovered that train travel surpassed anything I could have imagined
as a kid. Back then the train came and went, leaving us to dream of the days when we
could seek our fortunes elsewhere. And while fortune—gold, copper, and coal—is what
Alaska trains were originally built to carry, the experience of riding the rails has become
its own reward.

The Alaska Railroad extends for nearly five hundred miles on a main, single-track line from the
deepwater port of Seward to its terminus in the Interior city of Fairbanks. A 12.4-mile branch line

▲ *Train approaches Seward.*

▶ *A southbound passenger train crosses Snow River
near Seward.*

★

Train travelers can sit back, relax, and enjoy the scenery without worrying about road conditions or getting stuck behind a slow-moving RV.

▲ *A northbound passenger train wends its way through the Chugach National Forest near Seward.*

travels from the main track to the port of Whittier, a gateway to Prince William Sound. The only full-service railroad still operating in the United States, the Alaska Railroad provides both freight and passenger service year-round. In so doing, the railroad passes through some of the most spectacular terrain on earth.

Glaciers, jagged mountains, deep gorges, and expansive vistas pass by in a parade of natural wonders. Train travelers can sit back, relax, and enjoy the scenery without worrying about road conditions or getting stuck behind a slow-moving RV. The click of the tracks and the gentle sway of the railcars make for a restful pace, conducive to both reflection and discovery.

Just a few hundred feet from the tracks, fifty miles south of Anchorage, the Bartlett and Spencer Glaciers give passengers an opportunity to see the wrinkled, prehistoric masses of ice that carved much of this land. As the train moves through the Kenai Mountains, stunning views of deep canyons, still lakes, and braided streams fill the windows. The ride affords a tour of beautiful Turnagain Arm, a branch of Cook Inlet, while it parallels much of the Seward Highway, a National Scenic Byway. North from Anchorage, the route travels past the Matanuska Valley toward Mount McKinley, the highest peak in North America. Forest and the Alaska Range give way to a region known as the Interior, a landscape marked by great rivers and tributaries, lakes, and habitat for millions of migratory birds.

To lean out the open windows of the vestibule between railcars is to awaken the senses to the passing landscape. A summer breeze hints at the salty ocean air of Seward. The fragrance of fireweed and rain-washed raspberries wafts up along the tracks in the Kenai Mountains. Later in the year, cranberry bushes turn crimson and the scent of autumn signals the season's change. In winter, the air smells like crisp, fresh bedsheets hung outside to dry.

I have never ridden the Alaska Railroad without seeing animals, even in winter. I once watched four wolves lope alongside the train for several hundred yards before veering off into the snow-covered hills. It's not unusual to see moose browsing on willow and young birch beside the tracks—a habit that proves dangerous in winter, when the animals use the tracks as a snow-free trail, too often leading to fatal encounters with trains. Black bears, caribou, and occasionally brown bears also wander within sight of the train. Engineers often slow down so that passengers can get a better look. Train etiquette in Alaska invites passengers to alert other travelers to wildlife. "Moose, left!" can precipitate a mass movement to the left side of a railcar for better viewing.

Several specialty trains share the railroad's single track between Seward and Fairbanks. The annual ski train is a personal favorite. Twice each spring, the train takes skiers and snowshoers to a remote valley for a day of backcountry fun. The train serves as a warming house while skiers play in pristine snow. On the trip

The Alaska Railroad owns and operates:

- 52 locomotives
- 43 passenger cars (including diners, baggage cars, dome coaches, flat-top coaches, lounges, and sunroom table cars)
- 1,672 freight cars, both owned and leased
- The Alaska Railroad pulls 30 passenger cars belonging to touring companies.

Locomotion

The term "train" means the same thing to a railroad that "flight" means to the airline industry. It is more of a schedule than a particular piece of equipment. You wouldn't point to an aircraft on display at a museum and call it a flight; you'd call it an airplane. Likewise, the Old Number 1 on display in front of the Anchorage Depot is not a train. It's a locomotive.

Ah, Spring Skiing at Its Finest

What do a polka band, telemark skiers, and sauerkraut have in common? All can be found on board the annual ski train on two Saturdays each spring. That's when the Anchorage Nordic Ski Association contracts with the Alaska Railroad to take skiers, snowshoers, and other backcountry travelers into the wilderness for a daylong excursion into an area accessible only by train, where some four hundred snow lovers pile out and disperse.

The train lingers all day providing a warm place for people who don't care to venture too far from the tracks. Some folks bring portable grills to enjoy an outdoor winter barbecue.

Cross-country skiers and snowshoers have several options. When the train travels to Grandview in the heart of the Kenai Mountains, the Bartlett Glacier is an open, easy jaunt north with spectacular views of knife-edge mountain ridges. To the south, tucked at the end of a wooded creek bottom, lies the Trail Glacier.

Thrill-seeking downhill or telemark skiers can take to the mountains, but of course there are no lifts. It takes most of the day to climb three- to four-thousand-foot ridges. But the vertical plunge down thousands of feet of untouched snow makes every uphill step worth the effort. Another sweet spot for backcountry skiers is Curry, twenty-two miles north of Talkeetna, the site of Alaska's first ski resort. In 1923, the railroad opened the Curry Hotel, a place for travelers to stop midway between Seward and Fairbanks. The resort once offered luxury accommodations but in 1957 the hotel was destroyed by fire. Nature has since reclaimed most of the resort.

A charming tradition of the ski train includes a polka band, a railcar dedicated to dancing, and hearty meals of bratwurst, sauerkraut, and beer.

★

*Twice each spring
the train takes skiers
and snowshoers
to a remote valley
for a day of
backcountry fun.*

home, revelers of all ages gather in a railcar dedicated to polka music and dancing.

The flag-stop train that runs north from Anchorage, the *Hurricane Turn*, could be the friendliest stretch of track anywhere. This is the only train in North America that can still be flagged for a ride. With the wave of a white cloth, a traveler along the tracks can signal the engineer to stop the train for boarding. Likewise, when they want to disembark, passengers just tell the conductor where they want to stop.

◀▲ *The ski train affords
a rare trip into the best
backcountry skiing.*

◀ *Skiers wait to reboard
the ski train.*

▲ *Cross-country skiing in
Chugach National Forest.*

★

After a morning viewing wildlife, mountains, and glaciers from the train, the "Coastal Classic" arrives in Seward, where it shuts down and waits while passengers head out for more fun.

▲ *An iceberg lies grounded in Portage Lake.*

▶ *An Alaska Railroad train creeps along the canyon walls above the frozen Nenana River near Denali National Park.*

Many passengers on the *Coastal Classic*, traveling southbound from Anchorage, are headed for a day tour of Seward. After a morning viewing wildlife, mountains, and glaciers from the train, the *Coastal Classic* arrives in Seward, where it shuts down and waits while passengers head out for more fun. Some people explore this lovely little town, shop, eat out, or go fishing, while others opt for a half-day cruise into Kenai Fjords National Park to view the tidewater glaciers, otters, orcas, and other marine wildlife. All rendezvous at the end of the day for the return trip to Anchorage.

The *Denali Star* travels north from Anchorage to Denali National Park and on to Fairbanks, a trip that, weather permitting, treats passengers to spectacular views of Mount McKinley. In the park, the train stops at a depot just inside the entrance; from there buses are available to ride into the heart of the six-million-acre Denali National Park. Meanwhile, passengers leaving the park fill the train as it heads for the end of the line at Fairbanks—the northernmost train depot in the nation.

Alaska Railroad Locomotives Roster

Number	Locomotive Type	Year Built	Horsepower
1503	F7B	1952	1500
1551	MP15	1976	1500
1552	MP15	1977	1500
1553	MP15	1976	1500
1554	MP15	1980	1500
2001	GP38-2	1978	2000
2002	GP38-2	1978	2000
2003	GP38-2	1978	2000
2004	GP38-2	1978	2000
2005	GP38-2	1978	2000
2006	GP38-2	1978	2000
2007	GP38-2	1978	2000
2008	GP38-2	1978	2000
2801	GP49	1983	2800
2802	GP49	1983	2800
2803	GP49	1983	2800
2804	GP49	1983	2800
2805	GP49	1983	2800
2806	GP49	1983	2800
2807	GP49	1983	2800
2808	GP49	1983	2800
2809	GP49	1983	2800
3001	GP40-2	1975	3000
3002	GP40-2	1975	3000
3003	GP40-2	1975	3000
3004	GP40-2	1975	3000
3005	GP40-2	1975	3000
3006	GP40-2	1975	3000
3007	GP40-2	1976	3000
3008	GP40-2	1976	3000
3009	GP40-2	1976	3000
3010	GP40-2	1976	3000
3011	GP40-2	1976	3000
3012	GP40-2	1978	3000
3013	GP40-2	1978	3000
3014	GP40-2	1978	3000
3015	GP40-2	1978	3000
4001	SD70MAC	2000	4000
4002	SD70MAC	2000	4000
4003	SD70MAC	2000	4000
4004	SD70MAC	2000	4000
4005	SD70MAC	2000	4000
4006	SD70MAC	2000	4000
4007	SD70MAC	2000	4000
4008	SD70MAC	2000	4000
4009	SD70MAC	2000	4000
4010	SD70MAC	2000	4000
4011	SD70MAC	2000	4000
4012	SD70MAC	2000	4000
4013	SD70MAC	2000	4000
4014	SD70MAC	2000	4000
4015	SD70MAC	2000	4000
4016	SD70MAC	2000	4000

★

The "Denali Star" travels north from Anchorage to Denali National Park and on to Fairbanks, a trip that, weather permitting, treats passengers to spectacular views of Mount McKinley.

★

To help prevent untimely avalanches, crews shoot the snowy sides of mountains with 105mm howitzer cannons.

Along with passenger travel, the Alaska Railroad is an important artery for commerce in the state. Rail lines opened much of Alaska's economic frontier. In the twenty-first century, coal, petroleum products, gravel, and other natural resources still make their way southbound from Alaska's Interior to ports in Anchorage, Seward, and Whittier. Waiting at these ports are container ships with fresh produce and other products from the Lower 48, ready for delivery to all parts of Alaska by barge, northbound truck, or train.

Keeping the railroad's lines open requires year-round diligence.
Workers scramble all winter to clear the rails of ice and snow. It's not
uncommon for the area of Grandview in the Kenai Mountains to
get thirty-six feet of snow in a season. To help prevent untimely
avalanches, crews shoot the snowy sides of mountains with 105mm
howitzer cannons. After the unstable snow crashes down the slope,
crews go to work clearing the tracks. Rockslides and flooding test
the resolve of summer workers, who must continually build up
ballast and straighten the tracks. Yet in spite of Alaska's harsh
environment, freight (more than six million tons each year) and
passengers reach their destinations.

Some of the communities along the track, like Fairbanks,
were around before the train was built; others sprang up with
the birth of the railroad. The tent city that began as a railroad
construction camp on the banks of Ship Creek is now Anchorage,
Alaska's largest city. Nenana, whose population soared to five
thousand in 1917 during railroad construction, is now a quiet
community of fewer than five hundred residents. Talkeetna, once
an Indian village and then a camp for gold prospectors, is now
a staging area for mountaineers preparing to climb Mount
McKinley. And the bustling resort of Curry has disappeared;
a mysterious fire destroyed the luxury hotel in 1957.

A state-owned corporation, the Alaska Railroad is distinct
from others in the nation, not only for its far-north latitude and
its isolation from other railroad lines, but also because the state's
economic health depends on it in so many ways. As the Alaska
Railroad Corporation likes to advertise, the train truly provides
"the ties that bind Alaska."

From the tidewaters of Seward and Whittier to the broad river
basin of the Interior, the train stitches across a tapestry of contrasts
and extremes. For those of us who live along the rail corridor—
poets and painters, hunters and homesteaders, working folks and
adventurers—the railroad provides practical transportation as well
as passage to a place just beyond our imagination.

★

*Workers scramble
all winter to clear
the rails of ice
and snow. It's not
uncommon for the
area of Grandview in
the Kenai Mountains
to get thirty-six feet
of snow in a season.*

◀ *A freight train passes by
the edge of a recent avalanche
along the Chugach Mountains.*

Chapter Two

Welcome Aboard

$\mathscr{T}$HE ALASKA RAILROAD OFFERS SCENIC TRAVEL ON A SINGLE MAIN TRACK LINKING
Seward, a coastal community on Resurrection Bay, and Fairbanks, in the heart of Alaska's Interior,
fifteen-plus hours away by train. A branch line from Portage to Whittier, with 12.4 miles of track,
connects the main line running along Cook Inlet's Turnagain Arm to the waters of Prince William
Sound. The only other branches off the main line are a short stint to Palmer, where freight trains
load gravel, and spurs to the military bases in Fairbanks.

The railroad's hub and main depot are in Anchorage, with most travelers embarking here,
and proceeding either northbound toward Fairbanks, or southbound toward Seward. However,
tickets can be purchased to board or disembark at any of the train's regularly scheduled stops.
The Alaska Railroad offers several options for passenger service. In the summer, tours beginning
in Seward, Anchorage, or Fairbanks include scheduled stops at many communities along the route.

▲ *All aboard! Brakeman Rick Singsaas checks his watch prior
to departing Denali National Park.*

▶ *A Seward-bound passenger train runs along
the Turnagain Arm.*

★

*The dome cars on
the train are open
to all passengers for
a bird's-eye view.*

Tour packages can be customized to suit every traveler, from those who need wheelchair assistance to explorers looking for backcountry adventure. Packages often include excursions off the tracks: dinner theater, dogsled rides, whitewater rafting, and glacier cruises are just a few of the many choices. The most popular tour packages are highlighted on the Alaska Railroad Web site at www.akrr.com.

Full-service dining includes linens, silverware, real dishes, and a fully stocked bar. Chefs serve up a variety of fare, including Alaska reindeer sausage and salmon; custom meals may be ordered. Tour trains have forward-facing, reclining seats, and large windows. The dome cars on the train are open to all passengers for a bird's-eye view—no reservations are required. Tour guides simply ask that travelers allow others a turn in these cars.

Passengers needn't book a tour to ride the rails, however. Basic railroad service takes passengers to their destinations using the same summer touring trains with all the amenities. On summer passenger trains, high-school-age guides (most of whom grew up in Alaska) offer commentary all along the route, pointing out landmarks and the natural history of the area.

▲ *Passengers enjoy the Interior Alaska scenery from within a dome of windows.*

▶ *Passengers wait to board the Anchorage-bound train from Seward.*

In winter, passenger service is scaled down, with regularly scheduled service running only between Anchorage and Fairbanks. Except for private charters, only a limited number of freight trains travel between Seward and Anchorage between October and May.

While the distinctive blue-and-gold engines and railcars belong to the Alaska Railroad, other cars often tag along for passengers who are traveling with touring companies. Gray Line of Alaska, Princess Tours, and Royal Celebrity Tours all contract with the Alaska Railroad to pull their specialty cars.

★

While the distinctive blue-and-gold engines and railcars belong to the Alaska Railroad, other cars often tag along for passengers who are traveling with touring companies.

★

*During tourist
season, from mid-
May to mid-
September, the rails
are humming.*

▲ *Early morning passengers
check in at the Fairbanks
train depot.*

▶ *The snowcapped Chugach
Mountains dwarf a northbound
passenger train near Seward.*

ROUTES

Depending on the time of year, the trains of the Alaska Railroad offer varying travel opportunities and services. Passenger service all along the line is scaled down considerably in the winter. No passenger trains are available to Seward during the winter months; only freight moves between Anchorage and the railroad's southern terminus. But during tourist season, from mid-May to mid-September, the rails are humming.

Denali Star: This popular train provides Anchorage-to-Fairbanks service with stops in Wasilla, Talkeetna, and Denali National Park. The train runs daily from mid-May to mid-September, and has a full-service dining car, a dome car, and gift shop on board.

Coastal Classic: Operating between Anchorage and Seward, the *Coastal Classic* also stops along the Seward Highway for passengers headed to Girdwood. This train is often filled with cruise-ship passengers from Seward's Resurrection Bay. It runs daily from mid-May to mid-September, offering full-service dining and a dome car.

Glacier Discovery: For travelers headed from Anchorage to Whittier, the *Glacier Discovery* also makes a Seward Highway stop for Girdwood-bound passengers. The route uses the 12.4-mile Whittier branch line veering off the main line at that station. The train travels through two tunnels—one of which is nearly three miles long—before reaching the port of Whittier, with easy access to the fishing charters or glacier cruises of Prince William Sound. Since the trip takes only ninety minutes one way, it does not include a dome car or dining service. Baggage service is sometimes limited, so it's a good idea to call ahead if you plan to bring luggage other than what you can carry. The train runs daily from mid-May to mid-September.

Aurora: From mid-September to mid-May, the *Aurora* is available for weekend Anchorage-to-Fairbanks service with a stop in Talkeetna. The train travels from Anchorage to Fairbanks on Saturday and returns to Anchorage on Sunday. This route includes dining and baggage service.

Flag-stop train: During summer months the flag-stop train

This route is known as the "Hurricane Turn."

▲ *The Alaska Railroad's* Hurricane Turn *train stops at the trestle on Hurricane Gulch before its return trip to Talkeetna. Its run from Talkeetna to Hurricane Gulch serves settlers living along the tracks.*

travels daily (Thursdays through Sundays) from Talkeetna to Hurricane, a station at Milepost 284. This route is known as the *Hurricane Turn*. The Rail Diesel Car (RDC), a self-contained single-unit train, operates this route. No food service is provided and reservations are not required. Train travelers simply wave a white cloth to flag the train to stop. Passengers tell the conductor where they want to be dropped off. The flag-stop train serves homesteaders who live along the route as well as backcountry travelers who may get on or off the train at any point along the way. The train provides the only land access through this fifty-eight-mile stretch of wilderness.

In winter, the *Aurora* passenger train from Anchorage to Fairbanks offers flag-stop service on the weekends. The usual RDC train also runs on the first Thursday of every month. This allows residents along the route to make round-trip excursions over a long weekend; travelers can begin their trip on Thursday and return on Saturday or Sunday.

★
The flag-stop train provides the only land access through a fifty-eight-mile stretch of wilderness.

BAGGAGE SERVICE

Passengers may check two pieces of luggage, not to exceed fifty pounds, at no charge on most of the summer tour trains. Fees are charged for any excess baggage; oversized camping, hunting, or recreational equipment; and kennels. The *Glacier Discovery* to Whittier has limited baggage service; call ahead for details.

UNIVERSAL ACCESS

The Alaska Railroad has equipment to help passengers with disabilities board and depart the train. Every car has wide aisles, accessible restrooms, and ample room to move around. Generous seats and leg room make travel comfortable. Passengers using wheelchairs or other assistive devices are encouraged to call ahead to make arrangements for any special needs.

The Alaska Railroad partners with other tour operators for packages that include everything from helicopter tours to dogsled rides. Travelers can choose which tours best suit their interests and needs. Each tour has a designation indicating its level of activity. For the high-adventure set, there's rigorous hiking, whitewater rafting, remote fishing trips, and the like. Others may be interested in something a bit tamer, such as flat-water river trips, easier hikes, or bus tours. And passengers with limited mobility, or those who rely on wheelchairs, will find a menu of tours to accommodate their needs.

TO FIND OUT MORE . . .

For more information about reservations or tours, visit the Alaska Railroad Web site at www.akrr.com or call 1-800-544-0552 (TDD 1-907-265-2620).

Dynamite, Snoose, and "Big Mike" Heney

Two of Alaska's other historic trains—the White Pass & Yukon Route and the Copper River & Northwestern Railway—had several things in common. Both were built to transport the North's rich resources to coastal ports; both traversed nearly impossible terrain; and both were engineered by an Irishman who became known as the "Giant of the Rails." Michael James Heney, master railroad builder of the North, once said, "Give me enough dynamite and snoose and I'll build you a road to Hell!" (Snoose is finely powdered Swedish snuff, a smokeless tobacco.)

"Big Mike" Heney was sitting at a hotel bar in the coastal town of Skagway when he met Sir Thomas Tancred, a British financier. It was 1898, and the gold rush to the Klondike was on. But a mountain range and six hundred miles still stood between fortune seekers and their gold. Tancred and his party had already surveyed the area and concluded that a railroad couldn't be built through such rugged terrain. Heney figured otherwise. The two men talked through the night, and by dawn they'd made a deal. On May 28, 1898, construction began on the narrow-gauge White Pass & Yukon Route.

"Give me enough dynamite and snoose and I'll build you a road to Hell!"

Heney traveled by horseback, working eighteen-hour days, to oversee construction. More than 450 tons of explosives were used from Skagway to the summit of White Pass, 20 miles to the north. The 110-mile line to Whitehorse, Yukon, was completed on July 29, 1900—a testament to black powder and the power of Heney's determination.

Heney didn't stop there. One of the richest copper deposits ever found had been discovered between the Kennicott Glacier and McCarthy Creek. Construction of the Copper River & Northwestern Railway began in 1908, but not before Heney had convinced the powerful Guggenheim–Morgan Syndicate to buy his route and hire him as a contractor to complete the 196-mile railroad.

One challenge was figuring out how to build a bridge next to a glacier. It had to be done during the winter, when the glacier was less likely to move and temporary supports could be built directly on the river's ice. After the work was well under way, workers woke one morning to discover that the bridge was eighteen inches out of line. The glacier was awake after all, and the race was on to complete the bridge before it pushed the river ice and temporary pilings out from under their construction. Men worked around the clock in the dark and cold of winter until the bridge was finished. Just one hour after the final bolt was put in place, the ice broke free, sweeping the pilings away in a thunderous roar. The Million Dollar Bridge held firm; the race had been won. (Nature eventually had the final word when the bridge was destroyed during the Good Friday earthquake of 1964.)

Heney died in 1910, just a few months before the final spike was driven to complete the Copper River & Northwestern Railway. Heney's photo was hung on engine Number 50 during the spike-driving ceremony to honor "Big Mike" and his resolve.

Today the White Pass & Yukon Route is an excursion train with restored parlor cars that travel 67 of the original 110 miles between Alaska's coastal community of Skagway and Canada's Whitehorse, Yukon. The Copper River & Northwestern Railway closed down in 1939, a casualty of the collapsing ore market and the Great Depression.

Autumn spreads across alpine tundra at Thorofare Pass in Denali National Park.

Chapter Three

Dawn of a Railroad

$\mathcal{T}$HE YEAR WAS 1915—A TIME OF BIG IDEAS AND EVEN BIGGER DREAMS. ALEXANDER Graham Bell made the first transcontinental telephone call to San Francisco. Albert Einstein postulated his Theory of Relativity. Europe was in the throes of World War I. In Alaska, all that seemed far away. A wealth of gold, coal, and other minerals had been discovered in the territory. What was needed was a way to gain access to and transport these abundant natural resources.

Since the late 1800s, gold strikes in Nome, along the Yukon River, and near Fairbanks had fostered dreams of a railroad to connect the territory's interior with ice-free ports in Southcentral Alaska. In 1904, the privately financed Alaska Central Railway began laying tracks northward from the southern port of Seward. Carving a railroad across extreme terrain and weather depleted the reserves of even the toughest workers and richest investors. Within six years, the financially ailing Central was taken over by Alaska Northern, another private venture. By 1915, only seventy-one miles

▲ *President Warren G. Harding driving the "golden spike" at
Nenana, joining the north- and southbound segments of the line.*

▶ *A southbound passenger train from Anchorage emerges
from a fog bank in the Chugach National Forest.*

★

At the northern end of this vision for a railroad, a small narrow-gauge train was already chugging along forty-five miles of track that connected a network of mining communities to Fairbanks.

▲ *Engineer Frederick Mears and surveyor Thomas Riggs Jr. were principal players in the building of the railroad.*

of track had been constructed from Seward north to a flag stop called Kern—a far cry from the nearly five hundred miles needed to reach Fairbanks.

At the northern end of this vision for a railroad, a small narrow-gauge train was already chugging along forty-five miles of track that connected a network of mining communities to Fairbanks. The Tanana Mines Railroad (later renamed the Tanana Valley Railroad) hauled freight and passengers along two lines, one from Fairbanks to Chena and the other from Fairbanks northeast to the mining settlements of Fox, Gilmore, and Chatanika. The train delivered mining equipment and supplies to the settlements, and returned loaded with wood to fuel the train, sternwheelers, and the Northern Commercial Company power plant.

The question remained: How to connect the mines and communities of the Interior to the water ports of the south? The Alaska Railroad Engineering Commission, appointed by President William Taft in 1912, researched the failures of several railroads in Alaska and the scandals of private railroads across America. They studied the abundance of natural resources, Alaska's growing population, and the need for transportation across a vast wilderness. Between 1890 and 1910, the gold rush had doubled the state's population from 32,000 to 64,000 people. Even so, the population density of the state stood at 5,888 acres to each resident.

The Commission concluded that only the federal government, with the blessing of congressional funds, could build and operate a railroad across this wild land. And so it was decided that Alaska would have a railroad owned and operated by the U.S. government. The Commission recommended two possible routes. One proposed route stretched from Cordova to Fairbanks and used the existing Copper River & Northwestern Railway; the other route went from Seward to Fairbanks and connected the Alaska Northern to the Tanana Mines Railroad.

On March 12, 1914, Congress passed legislation giving Taft's successor, President Woodrow Wilson, the authority to build and operate a railroad in the Alaska Territory. Wilson appointed an Alaska Engineering Commission, composed of William C. Edes, who had constructed railroads for the Sante Fe and Southern Pacific; Frederick J. Mears, an engineer for the Panama Canal who had also helped build the Great Northern; and Thomas Riggs Jr., an expert surveyor and longtime Alaskan who would later serve as President Wilson's appointed governor.

The Commission reported its findings to President Wilson in February 1915, and in May, Wilson chose the western route from Seward to Fairbanks. Although the Cordova route was also viable, the Copper River & Northwestern Railway was owned by the

★

The Commission concluded that only the federal government, with the blessing of congressional funds, could build and operate a railroad across this wild land. And so it was decided that Alaska would have a railroad owned and operated by the U.S. government.

★

When word got out that railroad construction would start at Ship Creek, at the mouth of Cook Inlet, workers stampeded to the area.

powerful J. P. Morgan and Guggenheim families, who had been implicated in a national scandal that brought down President Taft's administration. Aside from avoiding political pitfalls, the Seward route also had the advantage of access to the Matanuska Valley coalfields, an abundant source of fuel that would be needed for railroad construction.

When word got out that railroad construction would start at Ship Creek, at the mouth of Cook Inlet, workers stampeded to the area. Almost overnight a shantytown sprang up with two thousand people living in tents and shacks on the muddy flats around Ship Creek. When Frederick Mears arrived at the tent city on April 26, 1915, his first job was to establish an orderly town site. In July of that year, the first sale of lots took place at Ship Creek and the new town of Anchorage was born. It wasn't long before the railroad camp developed into what it is now, Alaska's largest city. In 1923, the railroad's headquarters were moved north from Seward to Anchorage.

Building a railroad through some of the world's most rugged terrain was a daunting enterprise. It required more than just laying down tracks across an inhospitable land. The Government Railroad also had to create an infrastructure of work camps, supply terminals, oceanside docks, coal mines, and communities— complete with schools and hospitals. It built radio stations, put up telegraph and telephone lines, ran coal mines, and promoted tourism by building a resort in Curry, north of Talkeetna, and operating a hotel at Mount McKinley National Park. The railroad also helped to develop river transportation by running barges up and down the Yukon River from Whitehorse, in Canada's Yukon Territory, to the Bering Sea coast.

Much of the equipment and materials needed to build the railroad and its infrastructure had to be shipped by barge or steamship from Seattle, the nearest Pacific coast port. Equipment was also transferred north from the recently completed Panama Canal.

Many of the materials used to build the railroad were harvested from the land itself. At first, local wood was used only for pilings,

culvert timbers, and ties. Lumber for other building purposes was imported from Washington's Puget Sound. Eventually, sawmills were built along the route, and the lumber needed for snowsheds and other buildings became available. At the outset, coal for fuel was shipped from Puget Sound. Later, the Matanuska coalfields began supplying coal at a fraction of the cost.

At the height of railroad construction in 1917, some 4,500 men were working on the line. The railroad contracted with station men who, in turn, hired workers to clear a right-of-way for the track. When the job was finished, the number of yards that had been cleared was measured, and each man received a check for his share of the work.

Railroad work was hardly a way to get rich, however. Workers were paid about 37 cents an hour, just three dollars for an eight-hour day. In a five-month construction season, workers could expect to make little more than their boat fare from Seattle and the cost of room and board—if lodging was available. Many new arrivals had to build their own accommodations. The lucky ones

★

Almost overnight a shantytown sprang up with 2,000 people living in tents and shacks on the muddy flats around Ship Creek.

▲ *The tent "city" of Ship Creek eventually boomed into Anchorage, Alaska's largest community.*

Engineering challenges were plentiful along the entire route between Seward and Fairbanks.

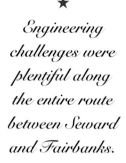

▲ *Building the span over Hurricane Gulch. The Hurricane Gulch trestle was built in 1921, boasts 100,000 rivets, and extends 915 feet across the canyon. The height from the rail to the creek below is 296 feet.*

found space in crude quarters with bunks called "muzzle loaders." The four-by-eight-foot living spaces were arranged like rows of post office boxes, with just enough room for a man and his duffle.

Events in Europe had a profound effect on railroad construction. On April 6, 1917, the United States declared war on Germany, and by June, American troops began landing in France. Railroad workers rushed to enlist. More men, per capita, entered military service from Alaska than from anywhere else in the nation. Even Frederick Mears resigned from the Alaska Engineering Commission to go to war, and with him went nearly half of the railroad's clerical and engineering personnel.

In spite of the exodus of workers, tracks continued to be laid down. Women took up many of the vacant clerical posts. Men who stayed on got a pay raise. The Commission began chartering its

A Bridge of Note

Although the Hurricane Gulch Bridge may be the most famous on the railroad—with its spectacular view of the Chulitna River and a creek that flows nearly three hundred feet below the bridge—the Mears Memorial Bridge was technically the most difficult to build. The bridge was named after Frederick Mears, Chairman and Chief Engineer of the Alaska Engineering Commission. The bridge, which crosses the Tanana River at Nenana, is seven hundred feet long, and stands forty feet above the water to allow passage of commercial riverboats. Foundations for the bridge were built in the summer of 1922; the bridge itself was constructed in the winter of 1922–23. After the river froze in the fall, crews drove timber pilings through the ice into the river bottom. These pilings supported the bridge as it was being built. The bridge was completed before the ice went out the following April.

It was at the north end of this bridge that President Harding drove the golden spike to commemorate the completion of the Alaska Railroad. A sign at the side of the tracks marks the spot where the spike was driven.

Along Cook Inlet's Turnagain Arm, more than four million cubic yards of solid rock had to be hand-drilled and excavated along the shoreline.

own vessels and barges from the West Coast. By 1918 the last tracks between Anchorage and Seward were laid, closing the gap that in previous winters required the use of dog teams to travel.

Frederick Mears returned from the war in 1919 and was appointed Chairman and Chief Engineer of the Alaska Engineering Commission. That year the narrow-gauge line was connected south from Fairbanks to Nenana. Slowly but steadily, the Government Railroad moved to connect the communities and dreams of the territory.

Engineering challenges were plentiful along the entire route between Seward and Fairbanks. Along Cook Inlet's Turnagain Arm, more than four million cubic yards of solid rock had to be hand-drilled and excavated along the shoreline. Eight and one-half miles of bridges had to be constructed across steep canyons and raging rivers. Seven tunnels had to be blasted through rock, and a roadbed shelf had to be cut along the side of the Nenana River Canyon. All of this was done with rudimentary equipment, and in temperatures ranging from more than 90° to minus 70° Fahrenheit.

In 1923, with the Roaring Twenties well under way, hemlines were rising, as was the ill-fated stock market. In July, President Warren G. Harding, accompanied by his wife and a large entourage of dignitaries, traveled to Alaska to commemorate the completion of the railroad. The dream of a rail line extending from Seward to Fairbanks had become a reality. It was a hot, sunny day in Nenana on July 15, when President Harding took up the maul to drive the spike that would officially complete the railroad. Harding, who reportedly had tipped back a few too many drinks before the ceremony, took three swings before making contact to drive the golden spike home. Visiting reporters had been told to wear heavy underwear, shirts, sweaters, and galoshes to protect against the cold and mosquitoes. Nenana was hot, and there were no mosquitoes. The next day at a speech Harding made in Fairbanks, several people collapsed from heat exhaustion.

▶ *Delicate beadwork adorns Athabascan footwear.*

Alaska's First People

*L*ong before the railroad broke trail across the wilderness—before Russian fur traders or prospectors arrived—Alaska's first people inhabited the land that Aleuts called *Agunalaksh*, meaning "shore where the sea breaks its back." One theory holds that 10,000 to 15,000 years ago, early people followed game across the now-submerged Bering Land Bridge that connected Siberia with Alaska. Descendants of these first people, the present-day Native peoples include Athabascans, Aleuts, Alutiiq, Eyak, Haida, Iñupiat, Tlingit, Tsimshian, Yup'ik, and Siberian Yupik. Each group possesses its own unique history, language, art, stories, and traditional homelands.

Traditionally, Aleuts lived along the Aleutian Islands and part of the Alaska Peninsula. Masterful seafarers, they hunted in skin-covered kayaks called baidarkas. On the water, they wore visors made of steam-bent wood to protect their eyes, and used harpoons to harvest sea otters, seals, sea lions, walruses, and occasionally whales. They also fished for salmon and halibut.

The Alutiiq people—often mistakenly grouped with the Aleuts—lived on Kodiak Island and some coastal areas of the Kenai Peninsula and Prince William Sound. Historically they lived in sod houses and used stone oil lamps to light their homes. Like the Aleuts, they were skilled hunters, using skin-covered kayaks to hunt for sea mammals, birds, and fish.

Eskimos—Iñupiats, Yup'iks, and Siberian Yupiks—lived along the coastal regions of the western Bering Sea and northern Arctic Ocean. North of Norton Sound, along the far northern coastline and inland on the rivers, the Iñupiat people took their sustenance from sea mammals, fish, berries, birds, and caribou. South of Norton Sound, in the Yukon-Kuskokwim Delta, the Yup'ik people settled along the coast and in villages on the big rivers. On St. Lawrence Island and Little Diomede, Siberian Yupik people live between the mainlands of Russia and Alaska. For all three Eskimo groups, umiaks—open-hulled, walrus-skin boats—were used to carry hunting parties in pursuit of walrus and whales. In these treeless areas, traditional homes were semi-subterranean, supported by whale ribs or driftwood logs.

Indian groups include the Haida, Tsimshian, and Tlingit people of Alaska's southeastern panhandle and the Athabascans of Alaska's Interior. The Haida, Tsimshian, and Tlingit enjoyed a mild climate and plentiful food, and they developed complex totem cultures rich in art and ceremony. The Athabascans were traditionally a semi-nomadic people who moved from one seasonal subsistence camp to another to take advantage of migrating fish, waterfowl, and other game. Athabascan people are further subdivided into several language and geographic groups.

The Alaska Railroad travels from Seward north through traditional homelands of the Alutiiq, then through the homelands of three Athabascan subgroups: the Dena'ina, Ahtna, and Lower Tanana people.

Each group possesses its own unique history, language, art, stories, and traditional homelands.

★

*"The Pharaohs
of Egypt,
in building
the pyramids,
faced no greater
difficulties and
hardships than
did the crews
completing
this project."*

▶ *The gandy dancers
from Cantwell were male
and female, including
Valdez Tyone, John Nicklie,
Grace Secondchief,
Lingo Nicklie, and
Helen Stickivan.*

The railroad had taken eight years and the influence of three U.S. presidents to complete. The cost came to $60 million, some $25 million over what Congress originally authorized. Shortly after its completion, the Government Railroad was renamed the Alaska Railroad.

World War II brought a boom in business for the railroad, but another crisis in manpower as men enlisted for the war. The railroad transported materials and supplies to build military bases in Anchorage and Fairbanks. The shortage of workers, however, became so acute that the 417th Railroad Operating Battalion was called in to help. Civilians and 1,150 military troops worked together to fortify existing rails and finish opening the tunnels through the Chugach Mountains to Whittier. In 1943 the Whittier line opened, providing a port of entry for all military cargo and personnel.

Following the war, after heavy use to build up the military in Alaska, sections of the railroad were nearly worn out. Congress approved a $100 million rehabilitation program to overhaul the entire line. Wooden bridges were replaced with steel bridges. Old, 70-pound rails were replaced with 115-pound steel rails over treated ties and improved roadbeds.

The Alaska Railroad was the only railroad ever built and operated by the federal government. In 1983, President Ronald Reagan signed legislation that transferred ownership of the railroad to the State of Alaska. The Alaska Railroad officially became the property of Alaska at a ceremony in Nenana on January 5, 1985. It remains the only state-run railroad in America.

The history of the railroad is a story of ingenuity and endurance in the face of unprecedented challenges. Bernadine Prince, in an exhaustive but now out-of-print history of the railroad, quoted railroad worker E. J. Cronin's comments about the magnitude of the job: "The Pharaohs of Egypt, in building the pyramids, faced no greater difficulties and hardships than did the crews completing this project."

The Gandy Dancers of Cantwell

Shortages of workers plagued the railroad almost from its beginnings. World War I saw an exodus of men from Alaska enlisting in the military. When the United States entered into World War II, Alaskans once again answered the call to battle. The Alaska Railroad was left with a critical shortage of workers, especially gandy dancers, a term given to track laborers who used railroad tools made by the Gandy Manufacturing Company.

The gold mines around Cantwell were shut down during World War II, leaving many families without a source of income. A group of Athabascan women—several of them sisters and friends—already knew how to use a pick and a shovel from their work in the mines, and they were willing to learn whatever it took to make a living on the railroad. Hugh Jones, a section foreman at Cantwell, recalled the women in a letter he wrote to historian Bernadine Prince. By his account, road master Joe McNavish hired them with one stipulation: "Send them in, but they'll have to 'cut the mustard' if they want to stay."

The women not only handled the job, they worked successfully on the line for six years. Grace Secondchief was as strong as any man. She became a legend, carrying ties on her shoulders and single-handedly loading heavy equipment onto trains. Other women were equally talented. Hugh Jones wrote: "No one could do as neat a job of dressing track as Helen Stickivan." The women were also good spikers, rarely hitting off the mark or breaking a maul handle.

Tough as the spikes they drove into the railroad ties, these women didn't put up with harassment on the job. One conductor had a habit of swatting the women with his glove every time he passed them on the train. Annoyed, one woman eventually grabbed the conductor's wrist and flipped him, head over heels, from the train.

Chapter Four

A Working Train

WHILE HALF A MILLION PASSENGERS RIDE THE ALASKA RAILROAD EVERY YEAR, FREIGHT trains are serving an important task by providing a supply line to industry and rural residents around the state. It is difficult to put a value on the role of the railroad—the transportation infrastructure it provides, and its impact on Alaska's economy.

Consider, for example, gravel. It would take sixteen hundred trucks to haul all the gravel that the railroad moves from Palmer southwest to Anchorage in a single day. Each day, from May through mid-October, as many as four trains made up of eighty cars each haul eight hundred tons of gravel forty-two miles from the mines in Palmer to the processing facilities in Anchorage. Gravel is essential for most modern construction; it is used for backfill, foundations for buildings, and to make asphalt for roads. And without the railroad to haul it, every mile of public road would be clogged with gravel trucks for four to five months a year.

▲ *An engineer waves from* The Spirit of Alaska.

▶ *More than a half-mile of oil tankers roll behind an Alaska Railroad locomotive on its way to the Anchorage yard.*

★

*Gravel is only
one of many natural
resources that the
train hauls along
its tracks.*

▲ *Oil tankers round a curve
near Nenana.*

▶ *A passenger train nears
Fairbanks at approximately
9:00 P.M.*

The Nenana coalfields hold immense deposits of subbituminous coal. Until 2002, the Usibelli Coal Mine at Healy extracted more than 1.5 million short tons of subbituminous "C" coal every year. For eighteen years, roughly half of it traveled south by rail to Seward, where it was loaded onto ships destined for Korea Electric Power Company. In 2002, the contract for Korea-bound coal expired and the Usibelli mine drastically cut production. However, together with the railroad, the mine continues to supply coal to six power plants that provide electricity for much of the Interior, from Fairbanks to Delta to Cantwell. Free summer tours of the mine are available by calling Usibelli mine headquarters in Healy at (907) 683-2226.

Railroad Lexicon

*W*hat's the difference between an engineer and a conductor? The rails and the tracks? Following are some basic terms to make sense of the language of the railroad.

BRAKEMAN: Assistant to the conductor. In the old days, before modern air-braking systems, the brakeman would have to jump from car to car to set the train's hand brakes. Today, the brakeman helps the conductor run the train.

BRANCH LINE: A track connected to the main line of the railroad. The Alaska Railroad's branch line to Whittier takes travelers through two tunnels, one a mile long and the other nearly three miles long.

CONDUCTOR: The person in charge of the train—the train boss. The conductor is responsible for the train and for passenger safety. The conductor also inspects passenger tickets. The conductor is qualified to perform any job that involves running the train. He or she is also a trained

Continued on page 43

Communications

*B*efore the advent of radios and computer technology, railroad workers came up with some innovative ways to communicate. Hand signals during the day and light signals at night let workers know—with amazing detail—what to do next in the process of running the train. A hand or light signal from a conductor could tell an engineer to back up, pull forward, or wait while the conductor moved between the cars. Conductors also used telephone lines to communicate. They could stop the train, climb up a telephone pole, and use a portable field phone to patch in to the nearest station.

Train whistles have been romanticized and written about ever since trains were invented. The train whistle continues as a practical form of communication on the railroad, a distinct code that gives the crew information about the movement of the train.

Common Train Whistles and What They Mean

* denotes a short blast of the whistle
— denotes a long blast

*	Apply brakes; stop
**	Proceed
***	Back up
—	1 mile from the station; test brakes
— — —	Stop at the next passenger station
— — * —	Crossing or bridge ahead

▲ *Engineer Chuck Tenney waves to a freight train on a passing track.*

▶ *A University of Alaska power plant employee shovels coal brought aboard coal cars from neighboring Healy.*

The railroad also hauls petroleum products, oilfield and mining supplies, chemicals (such as deicing fluid for airplanes), and heavy equipment for construction and drilling.

A railroad barge service connects the Alaska Railroad with the rail systems of Canada and the Lower 48—the Canadian National Railroad in Prince Rupert, British Columbia, and the Burlington Northern/Sante Fe and the Union Pacific in Seattle. Tracks laid directly on the deck allow railcars to roll on and off the barges. From Whittier, the laden barges are towed across the waters of Prince William Sound to Montague Island, where they begin a sometimes grueling, eighteen-hour push on the open seas to Icy Straits in Southeast Alaska. From there, mariners can look forward to the more protected waters of the Inside Passage to Seattle, where the railcars are once more rolled onto terra firma.

During the summer months, the railroad also feeds into a barge service on the Yukon River. The train takes cargo as far as Nenana,

Railroad Lexicon
Continued from page 41

engineer, brakeman, and fireman.

CROSSTIES: The timbers that support the rails of a railroad track. Crossties lie perpendicular to the rails on top of the ballast, the crushed rock that makes up the roadbed.

DISPATCHER: The person who controls train movement and work crews on the tracks. Dispatchers are like air-traffic controllers. The Alaska Railroad operates on a single track with trains that travel in both directions. Dispatchers keep trains from colliding.

ENGINEER: The person who operates the engine that drives the train.

FIREMAN: Assistant to the engineer. In the old days, firemen fed coal into the train's steam engine and tended the fire. Trains are now powered by diesel fuel. Firemen are still used as assistants to the engineer on long passenger trips from Anchorage to Fairbanks.

GANDY DANCERS: A slang term once used for railroad track laborers. The Gandy Manufacturing Company in Chicago made tools that railroad workers used to work on

Continued on page 45

★

*Beginning in 1923,
the Alaska Railroad
operated passenger,
mail, and freight
service as far west as
Marshall on the
Yukon Delta and as
far east as Circle,
162 miles northeast
of Fairbanks.*

▲ *A caboose trails behind
a line of oil tankers near
Anchorage.*

where it is loaded onto the waiting barges of the Yutana Barge Line.
River barges then take cargo to villages on the Yukon, Koyukuk,
and Innoko Rivers. The Yukon River empties into the Bering Sea,
and river barge service can connect with ocean barges to take
supplies around the northern coast to Prudhoe Bay.

The railroad's involvement in river navigation dates back to
1916. Docks and a terminal were built at Nenana to receive the
supplies needed to build the railroad. Construction materials were
then barged in from Whitehorse, Yukon, or through the Port of
St. Michael, Alaska, on the Bering Sea. Beginning in 1923,

the Alaska Railroad operated passenger, mail, and freight service as far west as Marshall on the Yukon Delta and as far east as Circle, 162 miles northeast of Fairbanks. Air travel eventually took over mail and passenger services. But the barge lines, now operated by private commercial companies, still provide a freight link from the railroad to remote river villages.

With ongoing efforts to upgrade its facilities and services throughout the state, the Alaska Railroad continues to transform itself into a more modern, efficient, and vital part of Alaska's transportation industry.

Railroad Lexicon
Continued from page 43

the tracks. Although most gandy dancers were male, a group of Athabascan women made up a section crew near Cantwell during the 1940s.

LINE: The course of a continuous track of railroad. The Alaska Railroad has 466 miles of main line, 59 miles of branch line, and 86 miles of yards and siding (passing tracks).

RAILS: The actual pair of parallel bars running along the top of the crossties. The width between the rails of a standard-gauge railroad is 56.5 inches. Narrow-gauge railroads measure 36 inches between the rails. The Alaska Railroad is a standard-gauge railroad.

ROADBED: The foundation that supports the crossties and rails of a railroad. The roadbed is made up of ballast—the crushed rock directly beneath the ties—and the subgrade, the leveled foundation of earth beneath the ballast.

ROADHOUSE: An old term for places that provided travelers with meals and a place to stay. In Alaska, roadhouses

Continued on page 47

Railroad Maintenance

If Alaska Railroad maintenance teams could call on divine help, they might enlist the aid of Saint Gregory the Wonder Worker—patron saint for protection against earthquakes, floods, and lost causes. Laying tracks across a wilderness back in the early 1900s was just the beginning; the geologic forces that shape Alaska's spectacular terrain also conspire to disrupt the best-laid plans to keep the trains on their tracks. Vigilance is the name of the game—inspectors continually patrol rails and bridges, alerting section crews to potential problems. Once inspectors identify a hazard, the work begins. And the work is unending.

In winter, avalanches thunder down mountain chutes and bury tracks with tons of snow and debris. Springs, creeks, and seepages freeze during the winter and glaciate across the rails. Frost heaves warp and buckle otherwise level tracks. In spring, floods wash away ballast and erode gravel embankments. Mud and silt from thawing glacial moraines slide across the tracks. Loosened by winter frost, rocks tumble from slopes and fall onto the rails.

If you compound seasonal difficulties with events such as the 1964 earthquake and the 1986 one-hundred-year flood that washed out two bridges north of Wasilla, it's no wonder crews grow weary. One worker said, "When I retire, I'm going to put a snow shovel on the front end of a motor home and head south. When someone stops to ask me what a shovel is, I figure maybe I've gone far enough."

"When I retire, I'm going to put a snow shovel on the front end of a motor home and head south. When someone stops to ask me what a shovel is, I figure maybe I've gone far enough."

▲ *Locomotives await service at the Anchorage train yard.*

▶ *A passenger train makes one of the last few bends before its straight run into the terminal in Fairbanks.*

Railroad Lexicon
Continued from page 45
included places along dogsled routes. In the 1920s, "Alaska Nellie" Lawing ran several railroad roadhouses.

STATION: Any designated place along the tracks; a reference point for train crews to mark a train's location. A station can be as simple as a signpost along the route. A depot is a type of station where people can buy tickets and get on or off the train. There are functioning depots in Seward, Anchorage, Talkeetna, Denali, and Fairbanks. The depot in Wasilla is currently used as a community center, and the one in Nenana is now a railroad museum.

TRACKS: The combined rails, crossties, and roadbed of the railroad.

YARD: Overseen by the yard master, the yard is the railroad center where trains are assembled, serviced, and switched from track to track. Here the cars full of cargo are disbursed to sidetracks, where they are unloaded by different industries. The empty cars are then reassembled into trains.

Chapter Five

The Great Land

$\mathscr{P}$ROBABLY NO WORD BETTER CAPTURES THE ESSENCE OF ALASKA THAN ITS OWN NAME. The word *Alaska* is derived from *Alyeska*, an Aleut word meaning "The Great Land." The state is actually a vast patchwork of regions bounded by geographic features that contribute to each region's climate, as well as determine what flora and fauna will thrive there. Traveling by train, passengers will see changes in the trees and flowers, wildlife, weather patterns, and general geography as the route transitions from the coast and glaciated mountains of Southcentral, through the Alaska Range, to the broad, semiarid Interior.

Most railroad passengers begin their journey at the Alaska Railroad's base in Anchorage. They'll choose the northbound leg toward Fairbanks, or head south toward Seward. In either direction, as the miles unfold, the differences between these unique landscapes and geologic features are revealed.

▲ *A northbound train from Seward crosses the trestle at Snow River.*

▶ *Spring greenery emerges at Thorofare Pass in Denali National Park.*

★

The "Coastal Classic" route hugs the shore of Cook Inlet's Turnagain Arm.

▲ *A couple walks along Cook Inlet's Turnagain Arm at sunset.*

SOUTHBOUND — The *Coastal Classic*

Headed south from Anchorage, the *Coastal Classic* route hugs the shore of Cook Inlet's Turnagain Arm, pushes through the picturesque Kenai Mountains, and descends again to sea level at Seward.

Traveling the tracks along the narrow, fingerlike bay of Turnagain Arm, it is hard to decide whether to look left or right. On one side, the wildlife-rich Chugach Mountains rise like sentries over Turnagain Arm. On the other, the churning waters of Cook Inlet give way to the second-largest tidal range in North America, with a nearly forty-foot difference between the highest and lowest tides in the Inlet. Only the Bay of Fundy in Nova Scotia exceeds such extreme tidal variations. As the tide funnels into the Inlet's Turnagain Arm, a wall of water builds up and rushes inland in a phenomenon known as a "bore tide." Each spring, when tides fluctuate drastically, bore tides can create a six-foot wall of water reaching speeds of up to twelve miles per hour.

Near Portage, a branch of tracks travels southeast to the town of Whittier. This line burrows through two mountain tunnels—one a mile long, the other nearly three miles long—to arrive at a gateway to the waters of Prince William Sound. While glacial silt gives Cook Inlet its murky color, ocean currents and a rockier shoreline help create the deep-blue waters of the Sound.

South of Portage, the train climbs from sea level into the glacier-clad Chugach and Kenai Mountains. Southcentral Alaska is home to one-third of the world's mountain glacier ice. Glaciers are formed when there is more precipitation than can melt in a season; the snow's weight over the years pressurizes it into dense crystals that flow downhill like rivers of ice. Portions of the coastal mountains have been ice-bound for more than five million years. Glaciers move forward like slow-moving bulldozers reshaping the landscape. When they recede, they leave behind scoured rock, glacial moraine, and valleys dotted with boulders, lakes, and rivers.

★

As the tide funnels into the Inlet's Turnagain Arm, a wall of water builds up and rushes inland in a phenomenon known as a "bore tide."

The High One

Mount McKinley and its sister mountain, Mount Foraker, loom over the landscape like mythical giants. With a summit of 20,230 feet, Mount McKinley is the tallest mountain in North America. Locals call the mountain Denali, an Athabascan word meaning "The High One." Enormous enough to create its own weather systems, the mountain often remains hidden behind a veil of clouds.

McKinley lures climbers from all over the world. More than twelve hundred attempt the summit every climbing season between May and July. Just over half make it to the top; the rest are turned back by severe storms, altitude sickness, treacherous terrain, and other hazards. Most climbers fly by small aircraft from Talkeetna to the Kahiltna Glacier, where they begin their expeditions. The climb from the Kahiltna base camp, at an elevation of 7,200 feet, to the summit, at 20,230 feet, takes about twenty-one days to complete. Since the National Park Service began keeping records in 1932, the mountain has claimed the lives of ninety-two climbers.

In 1979, the late Joe Redington Sr., founder of the famed Iditarod Trail Sled Dog Race, and Iditarod champion Susan Butcher mushed a team of sled dogs to the summit. The youngest female to reach the top, Merrick Johnston, was twelve when she climbed McKinley in 1995. In 2001, eleven-year-old Galen Johnston, who is not related to Merrick, became the youngest male to summit the mountain.

The Bartlett and Spencer Glaciers, both within view of the tracks in the Kenai Mountains, attest to the sculpting power of ice. Before the 1950s, the Bartlett Glacier blocked the current lay of the tracks. The original line avoided the glacier and other hazards in a section of track called The Loop. This engineering marvel crisscrossed the glacial valley in a series of trestle bridges and tunnels. Thirty years later, the Bartlett Glacier had receded a full mile, making way for the new tracks and the modern, more powerful diesel engines.

NORTHBOUND — The *Denali Star*

Departing from Anchorage and moving northeast on the main line, the *Denali Star* follows the Knik Arm of Cook Inlet. The Knik Flats preserve the dead skeletons of trees that once overlooked the ocean. The 1964 earthquake liquified the glacial ground, sinking the area more than four feet. Saltwater soaked the root systems of trees. What remains is a grassy marsh littered with the bleached relics of spruce and birch. It is a favorite stopover for migrating waterfowl and a popular hangout for moose.

The train continues north past Wasilla along the Susitna River Valley toward the Alaska Range. The Alaska Range marks the southern border between the Southcentral and Interior regions of the state. The six-hundred-mile range provides a barrier between Southcentral's milder, wetter weather and the Interior's dryer, continental climate, where temperatures fluctuate widely between summer and winter. The train follows the Indian River, and then pushes through a narrow pass known as Canyon before winding northeast toward Denali National Park and Mount McKinley, North America's tallest mountain. The tracks then hug the sides of the Nenana River Canyon, where rafters can often be seen navigating the roiling waters below.

North of the Alaska Range passengers will notice the mountainous landscape giving way to the broad river basin of the Interior region. Taiga, a Russian word meaning "land of little sticks," is composed of a boreal forest made up mostly of spindly

★

The train follows the Indian River, and then pushes through a narrow pass known as Canyon before winding northeast toward Denali National Park and Mount McKinley.

◀▲ *Mount McKinley.*

▲ *A northbound train hugs the canyon walls of the Nenana River gorge.*

★

*At first glance,
the tundra may
appear featureless
and barren,
but a closer look
reveals a surprising
diversity of life.*

black spruce. Taiga marks the northernmost latitude at which trees will grow. Some white spruce, along with birch and aspen, also grow in this area. Above the tree line, which is only 2,700 feet or less in this area, is alpine tundra.

Fairbanks lies in the heart of the Interior in the Tanana River Valley, and is considered an area of boreal forest. Much of the Interior region is categorized as "discontinuous permafrost." While the tundra acts as a sponge, the frozen ground beneath it resists absorbing water. The result is a land of shimmering lakes, braided rivers, and swampy bogs known as muskeg. With no place for the water to go, spring floods commonly create major problems for railroad maintenance crews.

At first glance, the tundra may appear featureless and barren, but a closer look reveals a surprising diversity of life. From large mammals, such as brown bears and caribou, to dwarf varieties of flowers and trees, the tundra hosts a varied and delicate ecosystem.

Protected from arctic weather fronts by the northern Brooks Range, the Interior enjoys some of the state's warmest summer weather. Fort Yukon set the record in 1915 with a sizzling 100°F. Average summer temperatures are closer to 60°F. Interior winters also produce some of the state's most bone-chilling temperatures. Because the Interior is walled in by the Alaska Range, which keeps warm ocean currents from moving inland, it's not uncommon for railroad crews in Fairbanks to go to work in temperatures of –50°F.

The tracks that covered more than five hundred miles of the Great Land end rather humbly in an unassuming rail yard in Fairbanks. Human creations such as the sign that marks the end of the line seem diminutive in contrast with the vast landscape passengers have just traveled through. Red fox occasionally scamper through the yard, another reminder that the train is but a small fixture in a place that resists being tamed.

▶ *One of many railroad
trestles spans a creek along the
eastern boundary of Denali
National Park.*

The Day the Earth Moved

On Good Friday, March 27, 1964, at 5:36 p.m., the convergence of two tectonic plates, the North American and Pacific American, resulted in fault motion across their boundaries just east of Anchorage. The result was the most violent earthquake in North American history and the second-largest earthquake ever recorded. The quake originally measured 8.6 on the Richter Scale—later upgraded to 9.2—and lasted a harrowing five minutes. Its epicenter lay just fourteen miles beneath the earth's surface in Prince William Sound, about seventy-five miles east of Anchorage and fifty-five miles west of Valdez. The earthquake caused 114 deaths in Alaska and another 16 deaths in Oregon and California. Most deaths were due to tsunamis, or giant tidal waves, generated in the minutes after the shaking began. The largest tsunami grew to a monstrous 210-foot wall of water in the Valdez Inlet.

By the time the rocking and rolling subsided, the Alaska Railroad had sustained more than $30 million in damage. Most of the damage extended from Anchorage south to Whittier and Seward. Much of the ground along the Turnagain Arm sank five to nine feet, with the muddy tidal flats swallowing up entire portions of track. One landslide deposited a section of railroad into Kenai Lake. Another slide pushed a large piece of track into the Turnagain Arm. Bridge after bridge, from the Matanuska Valley south to Seward, buckled.

The earthquake generated underwater landslides that devastated Seward and destroyed railroad facilities. The slides increased the depth of water in front of the Seward dock from 25 to 125 feet. Two of the three giant loading cranes on the dock tumbled over and disappeared into the waters of Resurrection Bay. Tsunamis ruptured petroleum tanks, and fire broke out on the surface of the water in what some say looked like a preview of hell.

Even after six months of cleanup, the shoreline in Seward looked like a railroad graveyard. Twisted rails dangled over the water. Blackened tanks scarred the shoreline. An eerie quiet descended on a town that once bustled with the sounds of ships and cranes loading and unloading cargo.

In Whittier, the scenario was much the same. Fire broke out from ruptured tanks, and one wing of the railroad station was ripped completely away from the rest of the building. The tsunamis in Whittier forced railcars toward the land rather than into the bay. Amazingly, the Whittier rail tunnels were hardly damaged and became a critical link to the community during the first few weeks following the earthquake. The intact tunnels allowed the branchline between Portage and Whittier to reopen before the longer, more extensively damaged main line between Portage and Seward. Whittier's deepwater port quickly became the supply route to Anchorage and the Interior for barges and ships that had previously docked in Seward.

Portage, located at the junction of the twelve-mile branchline to Whittier and the main line from Seward, sank nearly nine feet. A town that once lay at sea level was now underwater at high tide. Chunks of ice from Cook Inlet came in with the tide and battered what was left of the town. The outgoing tide nearly unseated the railroad bridge at Twenty-Mile Creek as it crashed against bridge piers and abutments. In a daring gamble to save the bridge, railroad workers loaded several hopper cars with gravel and pushed the cars onto the bridge with a bulldozer. The weight of the cars held the bridge in place, saving another connection to the hard-hit communities south of Anchorage.

The earthquake scrambled railroad buildings and the yard in Anchorage. Not far from the tracks a slide destroyed three blocks of Fourth Avenue. A slide on the hill above the rail yard broke a new school in half and engulfed railroad buildings and machinery below the hill. The accounting office was so damaged it that was trucked away as rubble, jumbling all paper records and supply inventories.

Following the disaster, railroad workers and the U.S. Army, Navy, Air Force, and other government agencies rallied to piece together the fragments of a splintered railroad. Earth had to be moved, tracks laid, and bridges repaired. Communications also had to be restored. Within days freight trains were once again moving from Anchorage to Fairbanks. By April 7, trains began hauling coal from Jonesville to Palmer and Anchorage. And by April 20—just three-and-a-half weeks after the disaster—the first train crept from Anchorage to Whittier on a temporary track.

"Temporary track" acquired new meaning along Turnagain Arm. Twice each day from May through July, the tide rolled in over the tracks, washing away sections of the roadbed. And twice each day workers repaired the tracks ahead of the next train. Bulldozers sloshed through water, pushing gravel up to gandy dancers, who tamped the ballast back in place.

It took more than two years to fully repair and rebuild from the damage done in the devastating five minutes of the earthquake. But as it had through the original building of the railroad, the Alaska frontier spirit, one of determination in the face of hardship, prevailed.

Twice each day from May through July, the tide rolled in over the tracks, washing away sections of the roadbed. And twice each day workers repaired the tracks ahead of the next train.

◀ *Evidence of the 9.2 temblor was written in the bent rails and unstable bridges all along the line south of Anchorage.*

▲ *At Seward, the terminus of the railroad was destroyed, leaving twisted rails dangling over the salt water of Resurrection Bay.*

Chapter Six

A Wild Kingdom

ALASKA IS KNOWN FOR ITS ABUNDANT WILDLIFE BOTH ON LAND AND SEA. Since the main line between Seward and Fairbanks travels through a wilderness that is home to many of Alaska's land mammals, train passengers have a good chance of seeing the North's famed creatures. It helps to realize, however, that the railroad slices a miniscule path through an immense area. Seeing wildlife depends on luck, sharp eyes, and attentiveness. The wildlife mentioned here represent just a sampling of what passengers might expect to see along the rails.

Moose

Weighing as much as sixteen hundred pounds, moose meander along all the major rivers in South-central and Interior Alaska, including the area around the tracks from Seward to Fairbanks. The males of these long-legged members of the deer family lose their antlers every year in December and begin growing new ones that, by autumn, may be wide enough to cradle a full-grown man.

▲ *Grizzly bear.*

▶ *Bull moose feeds at a pond with Mount McKinley looming behind.*

▲ *Cow moose.*

The females are smaller than the males and do not have antlers. They give birth to their calves sometime between mid-May and early June. It's not uncommon to see twins at mama's side and, on rare occasions, even triplets.

Within five months, calves grow to more than three hundred pounds. By the following spring, yearlings are chased away by their mothers, who will soon give birth again. The life of a moose calf is precarious; wolves and bears take a heavy toll on youngsters. Moose thrive best in recently burned areas where new growth of willow, aspen, and birch provides ample forage.

For centuries moose have provided Alaska Natives with food, clothing, and tools. Professional hunters once supplied moose meat to mining camps. Today, Alaskans and nonresidents fill their freezers with a harvest of six thousand to eight thousand animals each year. Meat from animals that die in motor vehicle collisions is donated to charity organizations for distribution to needy Alaskans. Close monitoring by state and federal wildlife managers ensures that the animal populations remain healthy.

★
*Another member
of the deer family,
caribou outnumber
people in Alaska by
nearly two to one.*

Caribou

Another member of the deer family, caribou outnumber people in Alaska by nearly two to one. Close to a million animals in twenty-five herds roam across the state. They are the only members of the deer family in which both the males and females grow antlers. Although bulls drop their antlers in winter, cows keep them until spring—an advantage for pregnant females as they compete for winter forage. These handsome animals are uniquely adapted to live in the North. Concave hooves—split like two halves of a moon—spread apart to support the animal in soft snow or boggy marshes. Their feet also make good swimming paddles and excellent shovels to dig for food in the snow.

The caribou's hollow hairs insulate them from the cold, and provide buoyancy as they swim across rivers and streams. Adult bulls weigh an average of 350 to 400 pounds; cows average 175 to 225 pounds. Calves weigh about 13 pounds at birth but double their weight in just two weeks. A herd animal, caribou continually wander the tundra in search of food: lichens, grasses, sedges, and the twigs and leaves of woody plants. A caribou herd can migrate as much as nine hundred miles round-trip between winter and summer ranges—nearly twice the distance of the tracks between Seward and Fairbanks. Train travelers may see caribou on open tundra near or above timberline.

▲ *Caribou bulls.*

Musk Ox on the Move

During an epic journey to a new homeland in 1930, musk oxen got a lift from the railroad, making them some of the railroad's most unusual passengers.

Musk oxen respond instinctively to threats, such as wolves, by forming an outward-facing circle with their calves tucked safely in the middle. This defensive strategy had served them well over the millennia. When human predators arrived on the scene, however, the tactic proved disastrous—the huddled animals were easy targets. By the end of the nineteenth century, the musk ox was extinct in Alaska.

In 1930, Congress appropriated money to reestablish the species. Thirty-four musk oxen were rounded up in Greenland and then shipped to Norway and on to New York, where they were held in quarantine for a month. From New York they were sent by rail to Seattle, and from Seattle they were carried by ship to Seward. In Seward, the animals returned to the rails, traveling on the Alaska Railroad to a new home in Fairbanks. Amazingly, all thirty-four animals survived the four-month journey.

After being studied in captivity for five years, the musk oxen were transported by rail and then barge to Nunivak, an island off the Yukon-Kuskokwim Delta in the Bering Sea. On an island without predators, the herd thrived. By 1967, portions of the growing herd were transported to Nelson Island. More animals were later moved to the Seward Peninsula, Cape Thompson, and the Arctic National Wildlife Refuge. The population of musk oxen in Alaska is now close to three thousand.

Qiviut [KIV-ee-oot], the thick undercoat of the musk ox, is one of the rarest fibers in the world. The soft, brown wool is harvested by hand-combing the animals each spring when they are shedding their winter coats. The average yield is three to five pounds of wool for each musk ox. Qiviut is spun into yarn and knitted into exceptionally warm scarves and other clothing. Wool is harvested at a domestic musk-ox farm in Palmer, forty miles northeast of Anchorage, and the Large Animal Research Station at the University of Alaska Fairbanks. Eskimos on Nunivak Island gather the naturally shed wool from bushes and tundra plants before hand-spinning it into yarn.

▲ *Musk ox.*
▶ *Caribou.*

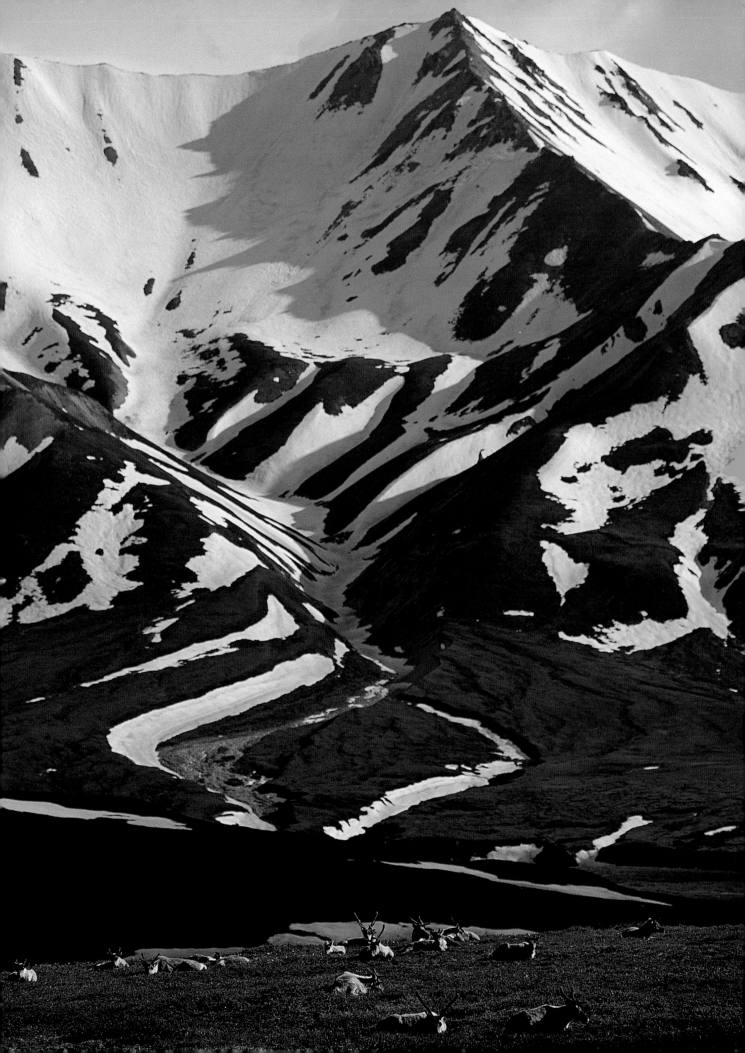

The Journey Home

*A*s the train traverses the 169 bridges and crossings between Seward and Fairbanks, an annual migration as ancient as the sea itself is taking place in many of the rivers below. All five species of Pacific salmon return to Alaska's waters each year, with more than 150 million wild salmon making their way from the ocean to the freshwaters of their birth. The journey can take them thousands of miles inland; Yukon River kings travel more than two thousand miles in two months to reach their spawning grounds in Canada's Yukon Territory.

Each species of salmon has its own timetable, which tells it when to leave freshwater as a smolt (juvenile salmon), and when to return there to spawn and die.

King *(also known as chinook)* salmon hatch in spring and live in freshwater for a year before making their way to the ocean. In the six to seven years before they return to spawn, kings grow into magnificent fish, often weighing more than 30 pounds. The largest king on record, caught in a fish trap in Petersburg in 1949, weighed 126 pounds.

Red *(sockeye)* salmon spend one to three years in freshwater lakes before moving to the high seas. They spend one to four years in the ocean before returning to spawn. All salmon undergo physical changes as they migrate to their home waters. The transformation of reds is the most dramatic. From their bluish silver ocean color, they gradually turn brilliant red with olive green heads. Mature adults average four to eight pounds but have been known to grow as large as fifteen pounds.

Yukon River kings travel more than two thousand miles in two months to reach their spawning grounds in Canada's Yukon Territory.

Silver *(coho)* salmon spend one to three winters in streams and up to five winters in lakes before migrating to the sea. Highly adaptable, silvers move to quiet side waters to escape spring flooding. In winter they avoid plummeting temperatures by moving to warmer, spring-fed streams. After just eighteen months at sea, they return to spawn, weighing eight to twelve pounds.

Pink *(humpback)* salmon are the smallest of Pacific salmon and spend the least amount of time in freshwater, moving to the ocean shortly after emerging from their gravel beds. "Humpies" get their name from the characteristic hump back and hook jaw that develop as they migrate back to their spawning grounds. These fish mature in two years and return home weighing about four pounds.

Dog *(chum)* salmon are sometimes called calico salmon because of the green and purple vertical stripes that develop as they move upstream to spawn. Like pink salmon, chums do not live long in freshwater before moving to the ocean. They live in ocean waters three to six years before returning home. Locally known as dog salmon, they usually weigh seven to eighteen pounds and, due to their inferior-tasting flesh, are often dried and used to feed sled dogs during the winter.

Dall Sheep

Dall sheep scramble on the cliffs next to the rails and highway along Cook Inlet's Turnagain Arm, south of Anchorage. Passengers are often surprised to get a close-up view of these rugged animals, just a stone's throw from the train. Dall sheep live in rocky terrain and high alpine meadows. They feed on lichens, grasses, sedges, and other woody plants. Ewes and lambs live together in small herds of six to ten animals. Adult rams usually keep to themselves except during the mating season. Both males and females have horns, but the males' are much thicker, curling as the animal matures. Horns can help determine the age of a sheep, both by a pattern of rings called annuli and by the extent of the curl. A full-curled ram is usually seven to eight years old.

Beluga Whales

Less commonly seen, but well worth watching for in spring and fall, are the beluga whales spouting and rolling in the waters of Turnagain Arm. Belugas are sometimes called "sea canaries" for their use of chirps, clicks, and whistles to navigate, find prey, and communicate. A beluga looks a bit like a snub-nosed, smiling dolphin, only bigger, with a bulbous forehead known as a melon. The whales are born dark gray in color but gradually turn white by age five or six. In spring, belugas chase migrating hooligan (a smelt-like fish) up Turnagain Arm. In fall, belugas feed on silver (coho) salmon moving from the Inlet into freshwater streams.

Bears

Alaska is home to three species of bears, but only two types are visible from the train. Polar bears live well beyond the reach of the tracks, far north along the arctic coast. However, passengers may catch a glimpse of a black or brown bear, as the tracks between Seward and Fairbanks intersect their habitat.

Judging the species of a bear by its color is not always accurate, despite the names. Some black bears have cinnamon-brown coats; others are bluish-gray. Brown bears, also known as grizzlies, range in color from dark chocolate to pale blonde. A better clue is the size

★

Passengers are often surprised to get a close-up view of these rugged animals, just a stone's throw from the train.

▲ *Dall sheep are visible from the highway and the railroad.*

◀ *Red (sockeye) salmon.*

▲ *Grizzly bear sow and cubs.*

and shape of the animal. Male black bears average two hundred pounds. Male brown bears weigh five hundred to more than one thousand pounds. Even more telling than size is the shape of the head and shoulders. Browns have a slightly concave snout and a notable hump on the shoulders. Black bears have more prominent ears and a longer snout.

Wolves

For as long as humans around campfires have heard their howls, wolves have been both feared and revered. Controversy still surrounds these animals as wildlife managers attempt to balance wolf and prey populations while considering the human harvest of big game. Wolves range over 85 percent of Alaska's 570,000 square miles. They are elusive animals; the best time to spot them from the train is in winter, when they are more apt to be visible against the snow. Wolves prey on caribou and moose and, occasionally, Dall sheep. Small mammals such as voles, lemmings, snowshoe hares, and beavers supplement their diets. The average pack numbers six to seven wolves, but groups have been known to grow to as large as thirty animals.

Sandhill Cranes

Close to Nenana and Fairbanks, passengers may see these birds that are sometimes mistaken for herons. Sandhill cranes are distinguished by their ash-gray color, bright red foreheads, and distinctive throaty call. Adults stand almost three feet tall and have a six-foot wingspan. Both stately and comical looking, they migrate to Alaska to nest on the tundra marshes of the Interior, the Yukon-Kuskokwim Delta, and coastal areas throughout western and northern Alaska. Graceful fliers, they take off in great circling columns, rising on warm thermals until they create V formations at higher altitudes. In one of the tundra's strangest mating displays, sandhill cranes perform a leaping, twisting dance, transforming these elegant birds into fine-feathered clowns.

This is just a sampling of the wildlife that travelers might see along the rails. The list of other possibilities ranges from bald eagles, marmots, and mountain goats to foxes and many species of migratory birds. Some passengers may be lucky enough to spot several different animals and birds in a single trip. Others may have to be content knowing that Alaska's wild kingdom thrives hidden among the foothills and forests, in the high crags and low marshes, of the beautiful land outside the train window.

★

In one of the tundra's strangest mating displays, sandhill cranes perform a leaping, twisting dance, transforming these elegant birds into fine-feathered clowns.

Wildflowers of the North

Wildflowers grace the landscape with startling intensity throughout Alaska's summer. More than fifteen hundred species of wildflowers bloom across the state. Land elevation along the tracks from Seward to Fairbanks ranges from sea level to the foothills of Mount McKinley. As the train moves north from Seward, the climate also changes from a temperate coastal region to the more extreme continental climate of the Interior. Differences in elevation and climatic regions, along with Alaska's perpetual summer daylight, make for diverse growing conditions and blooming times that vary with location. Flowers and plants that grow in alpine areas are smaller than the same species at lower elevations. The smaller, ground-hugging varieties better withstand colder temperatures, shallow soil, and high winds.

Following are a handful of common wildflowers that color the landscape along the tracks.

Wild iris is found in bogs and meadows and around lakes and streams throughout most of Alaska. The plant grows twelve to twenty-four inches tall and has a bright purple, violet, or blue flower. In June and July, acres of wild iris grow along Cook Inlet's Knik Arm, north of Anchorage.

Differences in elevation and climatic regions, along with Alaska's perpetual summer daylight, make for diverse growing conditions and blooming times that vary with location.

▲ *Wild arnica blooms at Stony Hill in Denali National Park.*

▶ *Late summer fireweed.*

Forget-me-not, the Alaska state flower, is found in alpine and subalpine meadows throughout most of the state. Forget-me-nots have short stems—six to fifteen inches tall—and small flowers, with five rounded blue petals joined by a yellow center. They bloom from May through August, depending on temperatures and elevation. Though they may be difficult to see from a moving train, these intense blue flowers are worth watching for when walking or hiking.

Arctic lupine often blankets entire hillsides with its showy blue flowers. A member of the pea family, this wildflower can be found throughout most of Alaska on dry slopes, in fields, and alongside roads and train tracks. These plants grow from ten to thirty-six inches tall and bloom from June through early July.

Fireweed, a prolific wildflower, is scattered along roads, trails, and mountain slopes from July through August. Its bright orange-red to purplish, spear-shaped blossoms bloom from the bottom of the stem upward. Local wisdom states that the first snow will arrive six weeks after fireweed blossoms "top out." These plants grow two-and-a-half to five feet tall and are often the first plants to appear after a wildfire.

Alaska poppy is native to central Alaska, the Aleutian Islands, and parts of Southcentral Alaska. The Alaska Department of Transportation has introduced Icelandic poppy along roadsides to revegetate construction areas. Native poppies are yellow or white, whereas the introduced species comes in a variety of colors, including red and orange. These six- to eight-inch tall, delicate flowers bloom in June and July.

Alaska cotton is actually a type of sedge with grasslike leaves and a seedhead that looks like a wispy piece of cotton. There are fourteen species of cotton grass found throughout Alaska. They grow from twelve to fifteen inches tall and bloom in June and July. Train travelers can look for these in shallow waters around the edges of lakes and in the peaty soil of wet bogs.

Chapter Seven

The Flag-Stop Train

THE FLAG-STOP TRAIN IS THE ONLY ONE OF ITS KIND STILL RUNNING IN NORTH AMERICA.
It serves as a supply line and transportation for the two dozen or so people who live along the
rails in the fifty-eight miles between Talkeetna and Hurricane. There are no roads in the area—
just snowmachine and four-wheeler trails. Only the train travels through this wilderness, taking
homesteaders to and from civilization, hauling their provisions, as well as taking adventurers into
the backcountry.

Mary Lovel wasn't quite sure what she'd gotten herself into back in 1964, when she arrived by
train in Sherman with four young children in tow. Sherman was nothing more than a flag-stop
144 miles north of Anchorage. Mary and her husband, Clyde, had agreed to finish making
improvements to a homestead just a stone's throw from the tracks. The homestead belonged to an
older couple who were anxious to move back to town. Clyde worked in Anchorage except for

▲ *The Alaska Railroad's flag-stop train.*

▶ *Mary and Clyde Lovel in front of their home in Sherman. "Sherman City Hall"*
was painted across the front of the house back when the town's population
was a family of six people, two dogs, and a cat.

▲ *Passengers and their dogs
wait to board the* Hurricane
Turn *train near Hurricane Gulch.*

weekends, so Mary and the kids went on ahead. The old couple had agreed to give Mary a primer on wilderness living until Clyde could join them, but it turned out that the ex-homesteaders couldn't wait to leave. They hopped the afternoon train back to Anchorage, leaving Mary and the children to fend for themselves. Before the train pulled away, they warned her about a bear that kept coming around to pester the dog. Best keep an eye on the kids.

With that, the Lovel family adventure began. The two-room shack had no door, so Mary hung a blanket. She lined the children up and they held hands as they trekked through shoulder-high grass to get to the creek, their only source of water. She found some empty fifty-five-gallon fuel barrels and had the kids roll them around the meadow surrounding the house. By flattening the grass, Mary would be able to see the children—and any marauding bears.

"I was sure if the kids stepped outside they'd be eaten," she remembers.

The beds they'd brought on the train lay disassembled with the rest of their things next to the tracks. The kids worked like troupers hauling gear and helping set up the beds. They ate like a small army—even the smoky concoctions that came off a dilapidated wood stove. Mary was a novice, after all. They had arrived on a Tuesday, and by the weekend, three weeks of groceries had been consumed. When they went to bed, Mary stacked empty tin cans on a pile of trunks in front of the doorless entry—just in case wildlife tried to step in for a nighttime visit. She slept with a gun.

The closest cabin was five miles north along the tracks, so the railroad quickly became their best neighbor. A section foreman from Gold Creek offered the family the use of a railroad phone to get a message back to Clyde in Anchorage. And while some women might have sent an urgent plea to get out, Mary's message was this: Bring a door—and more groceries.

"The railroad was our lifeline," Mary says, referring not only to their early days on the homestead, but all of the forty years they have spent there.

The train still offers not only personal transportation for scores of people traveling in these remote areas, but a vital supply line for fuel, lumber, groceries, and other sundries. The railroad delivers everything from dogsleds to doorknobs, dropping off pallets at trailheads that lead to people's cabins. Conductors of nonpassenger trains know to stop when they see an empty propane tank set to the side of the tracks. It's a signal for the conductor to pick up the empty tank, take it to Anchorage, and return it full. Conductors have even delivered moose killed on the tracks, knowing that any salvageable meat will provide a family with welcome food for the winter. Folks who live along the rails are on a first-name basis with railroad crews. Train workers often deliver the newspaper and news from along the tracks in exchange for a cup of coffee or a plate of fresh-baked cookies.

All of which adds up to one thing—the flag-stop train is rarely on time. But usually no one's in much of a hurry. The train is a

★

The railroad delivers everything from dogsleds to doorknobs, dropping off pallets at trailheads that lead to people's cabins.

How to Flag a Train

Stand with your gear about twenty-five feet away from the rails. Wave a large piece of white cloth over your head. The engineer will acknowledge that he intends to stop by sounding the train whistle. Do not approach a moving train—wait until it comes to a complete stop before boarding. Keep pets on a leash and use extreme caution at all times.

Note: If you wave without the white cloth, the engineer may think you're just greeting the passing train.

moving community center; people who live along the rails get on board just to visit with neighbors, who do the same. The train travels from Talkeetna as far as Hurricane and then turns around, giving friends a chance to visit before being dropped off at the trails that lead back home.

Deborah Lovel Bryner, Mary and Clyde's daughter, says growing up along the rails was great fun. She especially remembers the generosity of railroad workers. Her dad worked first in Anchorage and later as an extra crew for the railroad—a job that sometimes kept him away from home for weeks at a time. Johnny, a track patrolman from Curry, regularly checked in on the family. As a gift one year, he brought the kids heavy-duty snowsuits, hats, mittens, and boots.

"Johnny never talked about his family, and we didn't ask him a lot of questions. In those days, Alaska was a place people came to escape their past," Deborah says. "But we knew he'd had a sweetheart once. He was the most alone person I'd ever met."

When she was married, Deborah enjoyed a homestead honeymoon while the rest of the family stayed in Anchorage. She jokingly warned the family that if anyone decided to stop by for a visit, they'd be shot. That gave Clyde an idea. As Deborah and her new husband pulled around the curve on the train toward the homestead, they were greeted by a big white sign with red letters: "Honeymoon in progress. Trespassers will be shot." At first the newlyweds were mortified, but then they decided to play the part. Throughout the week, passenger trains slowed to a crawl as Deborah and Paul stood in front of the house, a rifle draped convincingly over Paul's arm.

When the Lovels and other families along the route say that the railroad has been a lifeline over the years, they sometimes mean it literally. Just add medical taxi to the list of services the train provides. More than once, the Lovels and other families have counted on the train to get them back to civilization and medical care.

In the Backcountry

$\mathcal{T}$aking the flag-stop train is a great way to access remote areas along the rails. But after you step off the train, you're on your own. Know what you're doing before venturing into the wilderness. And remember, the flag-stop train is rarely on time, so take this into consideration when beginning or ending your trip.

- Don't travel alone. Take a partner and let someone know your travel plans.
- Be prepared. You can't go back for extra food or gear.
- Dress in layers since the weather can change quickly. Wool and synthetic clothing keep some of their insulating properties even when wet.
- Purify all water. Most Alaska waters are as pristine as they look, but one bout with *Giardia,* also known as Beaver Fever, can make your life miserable for months.
- Camp clean. Avoid generating smells that might attract bears, including the use of perfumed soaps and creams. Set up the camp kitchen one hundred yards away from the sleeping area. Keep food in bear-proof containers and store them away from sleeping areas. In lieu of bear-proof containers, hang the food from a tree. Pack out all garbage.
- Respect private property.

Along with residents and visitors to the homesteads, the flag-stop train carries backpackers and other wilderness travelers looking for access to the remote backcountry. Adventurers are asked to respect private property, but beyond that, the wilderness is an open playground. Part of the track borders Denali State Park, an often unheralded but beautiful park adjoining Denali National Park. Rafts and kayaks can also be dropped off for float trips down the Susitna River. Conductors will drop off travelers anywhere along the flag-stop route.

Mary and Clyde are still year-round residents of Sherman. Their kids are grown now, have families of their own, and live in Anchorage, Eagle River, and Wasilla. The grandkids all know where to get off the train when they come to visit. "Sherman City Hall" is painted across the front of the house—a sign painted back when the town's population was a family of six people, two dogs, and a cat.

★

Along with residents and visitors to the homesteads, the flag-stop train carries backpackers and other wilderness travelers looking for access to the remote backcountry.

▲ *Conductor Buddy Gray assists passengers disembarking with their gear along the Hurricane Turn* route.

Chapter Eight

People of the Railbelt

$\mathcal{G}$ETTING TO KNOW THE PEOPLE WHO LIVE ALONG THE RAILS IS A BIT LIKE MEETING old friends. Most folks are quick to offer warm hospitality. Sharing stories around the campfire or the kitchen table offers respite from the rigors of living in a place that demands resilience and determination. People in Alaska are like people anywhere, except that they cannot help but be shaped by the remarkable land on which they live. From homesteaders to hippies, from prospectors to poets, no one can ignore the natural wonders that dominate the landscape.

Much of Alaska's population—nearly 75 percent—lives along what's known as the "railbelt," the string of communities connected by the route between Seward and Fairbanks. Folks who live here lead lives that reflect hard work, resourcefulness, and a yen for adventure. Here's an introduction to a few people, past and present, who've made their lives along the rails.

▲ *Gene Dinkel from the Matanuska Valley
with his giant cabbage.*

▶ *A traditional Athabascan fish camp along the Tanana River.*

★

Her lodge on the banks of Kenai Lake became a favorite stop for dignitaries traveling north on the tracks from Seward to Fairbanks.

▲ *"Alaska Nellie" Lawing made her home on Kenai Lake a roadhouse as well as a museum of Alaskana.*

Nellie Neal Lawing

In 1916, "Alaska Nellie" was the first woman to get a roadhouse contract from the railroad. She cooked for railroad crews, and in her spare time hunted, trapped, and ran a dog team. Nellie's trophy room housed an enormous collection of animals she had shot and mounted herself. Her lodge on the banks of Kenai Lake became a favorite stop for dignitaries traveling north on the tracks from Seward to Fairbanks.

Nellie Lawing's courage and grit grew legendary, with many of the stories recorded in her 1940 autobiography, *Alaska Nellie*. Once, during a snowstorm, she hooked up her dog team to rescue a missing mail carrier. After finding him near the tracks nearly frozen, she hustled him back to her cabin, where she thawed his hands and feet. Then she got back on her sled and traveled eighteen miles round-trip to deliver the mail to a waiting train.

Nellie faced one of her most memorable challenges with a
30-40 Winchester and a broken hand. Nellie kept a black bear cub
as a pet, and as she went to the barn to feed him one day, she noticed
Little Mike was missing. Following a blood trail, she encountered
a brown bear feeding on her beloved pet. The bear snarled and
charged, and Nellie hightailed it to the barn with the bear in hot
pursuit. She slammed the door on her hand, but managed to secure
the door just as the bear lunged against it. Eventually, the bear
gave up on Nellie and returned to its kill. As she waited for the
bear to leave, she grew angry. "The thought of the death of my
pet flared up all my fighting spirit!" she wrote in her book.

With her hand throbbing, she went back to the house for her
gun, then found the bear on a ridge above the barn. The bear
immediately charged, but this time Nellie stood her ground.
It took six shots before the bear fell dead at her feet.

Anchorage honored Nellie on "Alaska Nellie Day" in January 1956.
A few months later, at eighty-three, she died at home, surrounded by
her trophies and the memories of a life unlike any other.

Dave Thompsen

Dave Thompsen has worked a lot of jobs in his twenty-seven
years with the Alaska Railroad. He's worked as a brakeman, conductor,
yardmaster, and in several management positions. But none of his
jobs created memories like his seventeen years as a conductor—
memories and stories, he says, that could fill a book.

Dave was born and raised in Alaska. In 1975, while other
workers were trying to get high-paying pipeline jobs, Dave cast his
lot with the railroad. Starting as a brakeman in Fairbanks, he quickly
rose through the ranks and became, at age twenty-three, the youngest
yardmaster on the railroad.

Dave remembers the flood of 1976, when he and other railroad
crews worked around the clock, for two weeks, trying to push back
the Susitna River as it threatened to wash away the tracks. Some years,
the folks in Talkeetna would dynamite the river to break up ice
dams that aggravated the flooding.

★

*The bear
immediately
charged, but this
time Nellie stood
her ground.
It took six shots
before the bear fell
dead at her feet.*

▲ *An Athabascan fisherman
sets his net in Cook Inlet.*

Dave also remembers countless run-ins with moose. Train tracks are a convenient but potentially fatal walkway for moose when the snow is shoulder deep. Dave "moose shoveled" a number of the critters over the years. He would stand on the front ledge of a slow-moving engine, place the train's snow shovel against the moose's rear end, and push the moose off the tracks. He would then signal the engineer to highball the train past the bewildered animal before it could jump back on the tracks.

In the spring of 1985, Dave was headed toward Healy with an empty train to pick up a load of coal. As the train chugged toward Talkeetna, he heard the familiar thud of a moose strike. He radioed dispatchers about the accident, and the train continued on its way. Dave had no way of knowing that the dead moose had become lodged underneath the train. Shortly after the strike, as the train went over a road crossing in Talkeetna, the moose carcass wedged against the rails and began popping railcars, one by one, off the

tracks. It took four hours to clear the crossing of overturned cars.
In a snowy year when starvation, cars, and trains had claimed
many moose, the townspeople of Talkeetna cheered. At last, the
Goliath of a train had been toppled—if only temporarily.

Over the years, Dave added to his own experiences the tales
of old-timers who remembered the railroad's beginnings. In one
account, construction of the tunnels from Portage to Whittier took
a strange turn. A supervisor was puzzled as to why progress on a
tunnel had come to a standstill. When the supervisor went inside
the tunnel to check, he discovered workers digging at a gold vein
that had appeared in the walls of the tunnel. To the workers' dismay,
the supervisor ordered the men back to work and filled their gold
mine with concrete.

Twenty-seven years after Dave began working as a brakeman,
he still thinks that working for the railroad is a great way of life.
While his current job as fleet manager has him working in an office
in Anchorage, he sometimes misses being on the train—especially
the spectacular views outside the train window.

DeeDee Jonrowe

The full moon rises over the mountains. Northern lights, like
ethereal fireworks, reflect off the new-fallen snow. Big-hearted,
loyal companions strain at their harnesses. These are just a few of
the reasons DeeDee Jonrowe's life revolves around her sled dogs
and the Iditarod Trail Sled Dog Race. One of Alaska's favorite
mushers, DeeDee lives just a mile from the railroad tracks in
Willow, where she and her husband, Mike, train sled dogs for the
1,049-mile annual race from Anchorage to Nome.

It's a year-round, full-time job getting the athletes into shape—
only sixteen of their eighty-five dogs will make the all-star team
that travels across Alaska. On a typical training day, DeeDee gets up
at 6:30 A.M. and feeds her dogs breakfast. Then she comes indoors
to care for her other animals: four Labrador retrievers, three show
cats, and two guinea pigs. Eventually DeeDee eats her own meal
while sifting through mail, returning phone calls, and planning the

★

*He sometimes
misses being
on the train—
especially the
spectacular views
outside the train
window.*

★

In more perfect moments on the trail, when the weather is warm enough to leave her hood off, when the stars hang like jewels in the sky, when her dogs look at her expectantly, eager to run, she wouldn't trade any of it.

day's training. By 9:00 A.M. she has a team hooked up and ready to go. The trail takes them under the railroad tracks toward Willow Mountain.

Train travelers will recognize DeeDee's team by its mascot, a big, yellow Labrador named Parker, who accompanies the team on its twenty-to-fifty-mile training runs. Back home, DeeDee spends the afternoon as a sports therapist, massaging sore muscles and addressing any health concerns of her canine crew. The dogs look forward to a second feeding at 6:00 P.M., and then settle in for the night while DeeDee scoops the dog yard.

It's not an easy life, and the race itself can be punishing. In 1991, storms created a wind chill of –100°F, making simple tasks such as working buttons and zippers an ordeal. In those conditions it was difficult to cook dog food or boil water. But in more perfect moments on the trail, when the weather is warm enough to leave her hood off, when the stars hang like jewels in the sky, when her dogs look at her expectantly, eager to run, she wouldn't trade any of it.

Living in Alaska may have its long, dark winters, but the people of the rails would agree—the rewards of living in a place where mountains, streams, and caribou outnumber people far outweigh the challenges.

▲ *DeeDee Jonrowe, Iditarod musher.*

▶ *Conductor Buddy Gray takes in the view of Hurricane Gulch.*

Chapter Nine

Communities with Character

𝒯HE COMMUNITIES PERCHED ALONG THE TRACKS OF THE ALASKA RAILROAD RESEMBLE the members of a big family. Some are quiet and reserved. Others bustle with activity and ambition. And still others are like that eccentric uncle who no one quite knows how to figure. From small, historic villages like Eklutna or Talkeetna, to the larger urban areas of Anchorage and Fairbanks, each community along the rails has its own distinctive character. The towns described briefly here are ordered geographically, running from Seward north to Fairbanks. Although the train does not stop at Moose Pass, Ferry, or Eklutna, they are included as examples of communities with colorful— and sometimes off-color—personalities.

▲ *Woodland Farms reindeer, Nenana.*

▶ *Lakeside cabin in Hope on the Kenai Peninsula.*

▲ *The trestle along Snow River
located north of Seward boasts
some of the most scenic views
along the Alaska Railroad.*

Seward

The gateway to Kenai Fjords National Park, Seward is nestled in the Kenai Mountains at the edge of Resurrection Bay. Russians first settled the area in the late eighteenth century. The town was named after Secretary of State William H. Seward, who negotiated the purchase of Alaska from Russia in 1867. Fishing, tourism, a coal terminal, and the Alaska Vocational Technical Center provide the town's economic base. Seward is home to 2,830 residents.

Seward is the site of the famous Fourth of July Mount Marathon race, a contest that began as a bet between two sourdoughs more than seventy years ago. Today, the grueling three-mile competition draws runners from all over the world. Racers start on the crowded streets of Seward and then climb any route available to get up the mountain that overlooks the town. Coming down can be a calamitous affair as runners slide down snow chutes and try to keep their footing on loose shale. An ambulance waits at the bottom of the sheer rock cliffs at the base of the hill. Over the years, a number of runners have been taken off the mountain on stretchers.

The Alaska SeaLife Center overlooks Resurrection Bay and houses some of Alaska's most fascinating marine creatures. The center is a marine science research facility that also rehabilitates injured marine animals. Educational programs and exhibits make this a favorite destination for many Seward visitors.

Moose Pass

This mountain community, a twenty-nine-mile drive north of Seward, was first named in 1903 by a mail carrier trying to get past a stubborn moose as he was delivering mail by dogsled. A log cabin and log roadhouse were built in 1909 to serve as an inn and supply house for prospectors headed for the goldfields of the north. In 1912, it became the site of a railroad construction camp. The train began mail service in about 1927, with sacks of letters and parcels tossed haphazardly out of the railcar. Sorting and delivering the mail was sometimes left to chance, which prompted the ire of local residents. With the establishment of a local post office, the first postmistress, Leora Estes Roycroft, officially christened "Moose Pass," a place with more moose than people. Today, the community has a population of two hundred and is the site of the Annual Moose Pass Summer Festival, an event that takes place every June around the summer solstice. A sign next to a ten-foot waterwheel with a sharpening stone reads: "Moose Pass is a peaceful little town. If you have an ax to grind, do it here."

Whittier

A gateway to Prince William Sound and a launching point for day cruises, sea kayaking, and other adventures, Whittier got its name from a nearby glacier named after American poet John Greenleaf Whittier. The town is perched at the end of the 12.4-mile branch line that connects Prince William Sound with the main railroad line and the highway system along Cook Inlet's Turnagain Arm. The train to Whittier travels through two tunnels, one almost a mile long and the other nearly three miles long. The town was originally built

★

"Moose Pass is a peaceful little town. If you have an ax to grind, do it here."

▲ *Moose Pass canoeists.*

★

Anchorage has more than 162 parks. Moose and bears sometimes use the corridors that parks provide to meander through town.

▲ *Anchorage's visitor center is a log cabin bedecked with flowers.*

by the U.S. Army as a deepwater port and railroad terminus to transport fuel and other supplies during World War II. At the height of military activity, the community was a bustling town of more than one thousand people. The current population is under two hundred. Before the year 2000, the only land access to Whittier was by train. The tunnels are now a combination highway and railway, allowing cars and trains to take turns traveling the tunnels.

Anchorage

Anchorage, now Alaska's largest city with 260,000 people, sprang up almost overnight as a tent city of workers waiting for construction of the railroad to begin. What most historical accounts don't mention is how Anchorage really got its name. On August 9, 1915, residents were asked to cast votes on an official name for their new town. According to recently discovered records of the Alaska Railroad Commission, they chose "Alaska City." However, it was a moot vote. Someone with the U.S. Post Office had already dubbed the settlement Anchorage, a name used at the time by people on the streets and by the local newspaper, the *Cook Inlet Pioneer and Knik News*. The red tape needed to change the name to "Alaska City" seemed more trouble than it was worth, and no one really minded enough to make an issue of it. So the name assigned by an unknown postal worker stuck.

Anchorage has more than 162 parks. Moose and bears sometimes use the corridors that parks provide to meander through town. Bike trails throughout the city connect the wilderness of Chugach State Park with the urban setting of the state's largest cultural center. The city offers many of the attractions of a large metropolis, including a symphony orchestra, theater, dance, and other art events. The Anchorage Museum of History and Art as well as the Alaska Native Heritage Center are popular stops for visitors.

Eklutna

Not far from the mud flats of Cook Inlet's Knik Arm, through an overgrowth of willow and birch, lies the small Dena'ina village of Eklutna. Located about thirty miles north of Anchorage, just off

the tracks of the Alaska Railroad's main line, the Alaska Native community dates back to 1650. The Dena'ina people encountered Russian fur traders in the late eighteenth century and welcomed Russian Orthodox missionaries, who in 1835 established a mission in the village of Knik. Forty years later, the Alaska Commercial Company took over the assets of the Russian American Company. The Dena'ina people trapped and traded furs with store owners and the fishing vessels that had begun to fish Cook Inlet.

Today, Eklutna village, with a population of forty-six, reflects a unique blend of Native ways and Russian Orthodox beliefs. Colorful "spirit houses"—relics of Athabascan beliefs about the afterlife—rest atop the graves in the cemetery. Each spirit house is painted in specific colors to identify the family clan of the deceased. Each grave also features a Russian Orthodox cross. Centuries-old Russian icons are still part of today's worship services at St. Nicholas Russian Orthodox Church.

▲ *Anchorage's city lights against the Chugach range.*

★

*Wasilla was
reportedly named
after the Dena'ina
Indian Chief
Wasilla, a name
that is said to mean
"breath of fresh air."*

▲ *Christmas lights decorate
the Havemeister dairy farm's
tractor, Palmer.*

The train does not stop in Eklutna, but the village is a worthwhile destination for travelers who can drive the thirty miles north from Anchorage.

Wasilla

Home of the Iditarod Trail Sled Dog Race headquarters, Wasilla was established in 1917 at the intersection of a mining trail and the newly constructed railroad. In March of every year, mushers and their dog teams head from downtown Anchorage to make their way over 1,049 miles of wilderness terrain to Nome. The race commemorates the serum run of 1925, when dog teams delivered diphtheria serum to the epidemic-stricken Nome, a town on the Bering Sea coast. The race from Anchorage to Eagle River is a ceremonial beginning. The race clock actually starts in Wasilla one day later.

Another attraction in Wasilla is the Museum of Alaska Transportation and Industry. This impressive rail collection, primarily from the Alaska Railroad, includes diesel locomotives, World War II troop cars converted into box cars, a steam locomotive, a crane, and other treats for train fans and history buffs.

Wasilla has 5,500 residents and lies forty-three miles north of Anchorage. The town was reportedly named after the Dena'ina Indian Chief Wasilla, a name that is said to mean "breath of fresh air."

Talkeetna

Talkeetna is home to an interesting—some would say quirky—mix of characters, among them hippies, homesteaders, miners, climbers, and artists. Settled in about 1900 by gold prospectors and trappers, Talkeetna lies at the junction of the Talkeetna, Susitna, and Chulitna Rivers, a launching point for fishing or float-trip adventurers.

Artists find inspiration in its spectacular views of Mount McKinley, and climbers head to Talkeetna from all over the world to begin their expeditions on North America's tallest peak. The mountain is sixty miles away, a twenty-five-minute plane ride. History buffs enjoy the inn that hosted President and Mrs. Harding when they came to Alaska in 1923, and the Moose Dropping Festival draws in the fun-loving and the curious. The annual Wilderness Women Contest and bachelor auction liven up December as women compete to prove their toughness. The fund-raiser features events such as hunting, fishing, hauling water without spilling, and making sandwiches in below-zero temperatures. The sandwiches and an open beer are then "delivered" to a reclining bachelor—unceremoniously in his lap.

Ferry

Ferry can hardly be considered a town, with just twenty-five residents living along the main line of the railroad tracks. But it has a mayor, even though there's never been an election. Its post office, built in 1910, now serves as a dilapidated pool hall. Ferry's claim to fame is its Fourth of July celebration, hosted by its self-appointed mayor. The highlight of the party is the 5:00 P.M. northbound passenger train. As it passes through, residents line up to moon the train, giving tourists a look at a real "bare." Some might call such revelry a different form of Alaska crude. To the relief of most passengers, the train does not stop here.

Nenana

Nenana, population 435, is located on the south bank of the Tanana River, just east of the mouth of the Nenana River. Its location provided an important transportation link long before the gold rush or the railroad. Athabascan Indians once traveled the Tanana River to the village of Tanana, where they bartered with other Natives and Russian fur traders. It was in Nenana that President Warren G. Harding drove the golden spike commemorating the completion of the railroad in 1923.

Nenana is a railroad stop and home of the annual Nenana Ice Classic. Vying for a pool of $300,000, people across the state can lay out $2 a try to guess the exact time, to the nearest minute, that the Tanana River ice will break up and begin to move.

The train depot at Nenana is listed on the National Register of Historic Places. It was built in 1923, renovated in 1988, and is now the site of the Alaska Railroad Museum.

Nenana Ice Classic

While building a bridge across the Tanana River in 1917, Alaska Railroad workers made a bet on the date and time the river ice would break up. The first pool was $800, and since then the contest has become an annual statewide event. The contest is based on guessing when the ice in the river will melt enough to move a log "tripod" 100 feet downriver. The four-legged "tripod" is planted in the ice with a wire attached from the top to a watchtower on shore. The watchtower, in turn, is rigged to a clock that stops when the tripod moves 100 feet. A siren signals the first movement, and residents rush to the riverbank to watch as the tripod moves, the ice begins to surge, and the river opens up for spring.

Today, the pool offers $300,000 in cash to the winner or winners who guess the exact time, to the nearest minute, of the Tanana River's official breakup—sometime between April 20 and May 20 each spring.

Fairbanks

Known as Alaska's Golden Heart City, Fairbanks is Alaska's second-largest metropolis, with a population of 35,000. Captain E. T. Barnette established a trading post on the Chena River here in 1901. His goal had been to set up a trading post at Tanana Crossing, but the sternwheeler on which he was traveling could not navigate the shallow, fast-moving waters of the Tanana River beyond the Chena. The captain dropped Barnette and his gear off near the present site of Fairbanks's First Avenue and Cushman Street. A year later, Felix Pedro discovered gold sixteen miles north of Barnette's temporary post. As prospectors flooded into the area, Barnette abandoned his original plan to go to Tanana Crossing. A town grew up around his trading post, and he became the first mayor of Fairbanks in 1903.

President Harding's railcar is on exhibit at Alaskaland Pioneer Park here. The park is also home to the renovated SS *Nenana*, the largest sternwheeler built west of the Mississippi.

▲ *Trumpeter swans at Creamer's Field Migratory Waterfowl Refuge, Fairbanks.*

▶ *Sunflowers at the University of Alaska Experimental Farm bloom at 9 P.M. near Fairbanks.*

On the campus of the University of Alaska Fairbanks is Constitution Hall, where the territory's leaders met to frame a constitution on the road to statehood. The University of Alaska Museum is a popular attraction that showcases, among other things, Alaska Native culture, fist-sized gold nuggets, and exhibits on Alaska's dinosaurs. UAF also offers tours of its Georgeson Botanical Garden, large-animal research station with musk oxen and caribou, and international arctic research center.

The World Eskimo and Indian Olympics are held in Fairbanks, as are Golden Days, a ten-day party celebrating the discovery of gold in the region. ★

★

The University of Alaska Museum is a popular attraction that showcases, among other things, Alaska Native culture, fist-sized gold nuggets, and exhibits on Alaska's dinosaurs.

Recommended Reading

The Alaska Almanac: Facts About Alaska, 26th ed. Portland, Ore.: Alaska Northwest Books, 2002.

Alaska Geographic Society. *Alaska's Railroads*, vol. 19, no. 4, 1992.

Brovald, Ken C. *Alaska's Wilderness Rails: From the Taiga to the Tundra*. Missoula, Mont.: Pictorial Histories Publishing, 1982.

Brown, Tricia. *Fairbanks: Alaska's Heart of Gold*. Portland, Ore.: Alaska Northwest Books, 2000.

Clifford, Howard. *Rails North: The Railroads of Alaska and the Yukon*. Seattle: Superior Publishing, 1981.

_____. *Doing the White Pass: The Story of the White Pass & Yukon Route and the Klondike Gold Rush*. Seattle: Sourdough Enterprises, 1983.

Cohen, Stan. *Rails Across the Tundra*. Missoula, Mont.: Pictorial Histories Publishing, 2001.

Ewing, Susan. *The Great Alaska Nature Factbook*. Portland, Ore.: Alaska Northwest Books, 1996.

Fitch, Edwin M. *The Alaska Railroad*. New York: Frederick A. Praeger Publishers, 1967.

Janson, Lone E. *The Copper Spike*. Anchorage: Alaska Northwest Publishing Co., 1975.

Langdon, Steve J. *The Native People of Alaska*. Anchorage: Greatland Graphics, 1993.

Lawing, Nellie Neal. *Alaska Nellie*. Seattle: Chieftain Press, 1953.

Pratt, Verna. *Field Guide to Alaskan Wildflowers*. Anchorage: Alaskakrafts, 1989.

Prince, Bernadine LeMay. *The Alaska Railroad in Pictures*. Anchorage: Ken Wray's Print Shop, 1964.

Ritter, Harry. *Alaska's History: The People, Land, and Events of the North Country*. Portland, Ore.: Alaska Northwest Books, 1997.

Romano-Lax, Andromeda. *Alaska's Kenai Peninsula*. Portland, Ore.: Alaska Northwest Books, 2001.

Tower, Elizabeth. *Anchorage: From Its Humble Origins As a Railroad Construction Camp*. City History Series. Seattle: Epicenter Press, 1999.

Wilson, Henry William. *Railroad in the Clouds: The Alaska Railroad in the Age of Steam, 1914–1945*. Boulder, Colo.: Pruett Publishing, 1977.

▶ ▶ *A sign in Fairbanks marks the terminus of passenger service on the Alaska Railroad, the northernmost railroad in North America.*

Index